More Good Words

Practical Activities for Mourning

Beth L. Hewett, Ph.D.

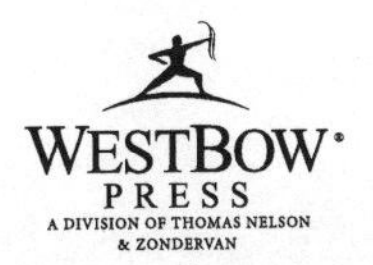

Updated 2014
Previously published by Grief Illustrated Press, 2012

WestBow Press books may be ordered through booksellers or by contacting:

WestBow Press
A Division of Thomas Nelson & Zondervan
1663 Liberty Drive
Bloomington, IN 47403
www.westbowpress.com
1 (866) 928-1240

ISBN: 978-1-4908-3809-0 (sc)
ISBN: 978-1-4908-3810-6 (hc)
ISBN: 978-1-4908-3808-3 (e)

Library of Congress Control Number: 2014909627

Printed in the United States of America.

WestBow Press rev. date: 06/24/2014

Beth Hewett has written an essential book on dealing with the loss of loved ones. ***More Good Words*** explores the crucial distinction between grief and mourning. She describes the healing that can come from mourning and five separate aspects to mourning. The book includes helpful exercises, questions, and activities to facilitate the healing power of mourning. I have known Dr. Hewett for many years, and the book captures her deep caring for those who have lost loved ones as well as her keen intellect and superb writing skills. I strongly recommend this book as well as her first (***Good Words: Memorializing Through a Eulogy***) for anyone dealing with death and loss.

Franklin W. Ellis, LCSW-C

In this heartfelt volume, Beth Hewett shares her experiences with death and dying, and with grief and mourning. Having lived through an extraordinary amount of personal loss, as well as helping numerous others to deal with their losses, Beth's insights are valuable for both the bereaved and those who work with the bereaved.

Deborah Czawlytko,
RN, BSN, MA, Parish Nurse/Pastoral Associate

More Good Words is a book for everyone who has grieved or who will grieve. Beautifully written, it is practical yet personal, and it addresses the nuances of grief. Read it at one sitting or a little at a time, but read it!

Tracey Eberhardt, RN, MS,
Faith Community Nurse, Bereavement Facilitator

Acknowledgements

As I wrote this book, I used a lot of experiences and examples from my personal life to supplement my studies of grief and mourning. After a lot of internal debate, I decided that including such intimate, detailed, and honest information would help my fellow bereaved readers the most. My family most graciously has supported my decision to self-disclose such information as it appears here. However, these words represent my experiences and point of view and not necessarily those of my family. I thank them for their generosity.

I am especially thankful to my mother Daryl who explored ideas and planned this book with me; she then took over some of my daily tasks so I could write it. Mom's grief journey has been exceptionally challenging, yet she has grown in beauty, love, and acceptance as she has walked her difficult path. She is my dearest hero.

I thank Susan Pahl for her thoughtfully written preface. As both a professional counselor and a dear friend who works with grieving children daily, her views are especially important to me.

Franklin "Skip" W. Ellis, Debbie Czawlytko, and Tracey Eberhardt offered their time and energy as readers for drafts of this book. Their comments and ideas vastly improved my efforts. I offer many thanks also to my husband Paul, son Russ, and daughter-in-law Tara who also have read drafts of the book and helped me to refine wording and imagery. Others who have read and commented on drafts include Christina Lengyel, Rick Ottenstein, Dawn Hammerbacher, and Chris Painton.

Photographs were provided by Robin Sommers, Russell J. Hewett, Bowen Lee, and Dawn Hammerbacher. Moonjoo and Esther Lee each provided original artwork, as did Virginia Lee Lengyel.

Debbie and Paul Gilbert graciously loaned me their beach house as a writing place, and I am grateful for their generosity and interest in this project.

A big "thank you" must go to Debbie Czawlytko and Pat Ourednik, my bereavement co-facilitators. As a Pastoral Associate and Parish Nurse, Debbie has given her life to the service of others, and she has been extremely generous in teaching me about the blessings of sitting with the dying as they reach the end of their lives on Earth. She has the most wonderful way of encouraging the bereaved who share their grief with her. Pat walked the journey of ALS, also known as Lou Gehrig's Disease, with her beloved husband, and she has taught me about courage in the face of her loss. Pat gives of herself freely and seems to become more whole whenever she gives. Both have encouraged me in my own journey of grief and working with the bereaved. Thanks also to Carol Hartman and Charlotte Crouse, who have shared their grief *and* hope with me.

I deeply appreciate the efforts of Robbin Warner, Ph.D., my generous and thoughtful editor.

Finally, I have deep gratitude for Dr. Alan Wolfelt's heart-based and intelligent seminars and books; he has modeled for me kindness, tact, and humility. Between him and my other grief teachers, I have learned to be a compassionate grief counselor who listen with both ears open, mouth closed, and presence available.

Dedication

This book is dedicated to the grief support group and seminar members who have bravely shared their lives and losses with me and with each other. There have been many of you throughout the past ten years—teaching me so much about your grief and lives with your loved ones. Bereaved parents and grandparents, children and grandchildren, spouses, siblings, and friends—your grief journeys have demonstrated that setting the intention to heal makes all the difference. I see your faces expressing deepest sorrow and learning to laugh again. I see you helping others in the groups. I see earnest sharing of sadness, anger, pain, defeat, and hope. You have demonstrated the beauty of living with and working through the most difficult of times. From you, I have learned to be a better spouse, mother, child, and friend. In my mind and heart, I name you and see your faces as I write this dedication. Thank you.

Preface

Becoming

A clay pot sitting in the sun will always be a clay pot.

It has to go through the white heat of the furnace to become porcelain.

Mildred Witte Stouven

I am honored that Beth has asked me to write this preface. As a lifelong friend, she knows I have dealt with grief often, both personally and professionally as a family therapist and school counselor.

More Good Words: A Practical Guide to Remembering Our Loved Ones is a welcome oasis for those who are grieving. With sensitivity and understanding, Beth makes the difficult feelings of grief acceptable. The activities and rituals provide us with practical ways to heal our grief, enabling us to look toward the future with renewed hope.

When we actively take control of our grief through intentional actions (mourning), we are able to move from a position of hopelessness caused by a significant loss, as in the death of a loved one, to a place of hope and healing. However, the activities presented are applicable to any significant loss, such as divorce, incarceration, or when close bonds of friendship have been severed.

Some will find solace and healing in centuries-old activities, for instance, weaving a grave blanket or creating a tear jar. Others will find healing in more contemporary ways, perhaps writing a "call and response" journal or using today's technology and social network. The activities may be used as presented, or modified in any way that is healing for you.

Mourning is about healing one's self. It is a very personal journey, often with many twists and turns. Whether you are just starting, or are further along this journey, *More Good Words: A Practical Guide to Remembering Our Loved Ones* is a book that can help you move forward with renewed hope.

Sue Pahl, LCSW-C, M.Ed.

Contents

Introduction

I am sitting in Paul and Deb's house, childhood friends who have lent me their beach home in Longboat Key, Florida. Their generosity has provided respite from the daily world, allowing me to write this book for you, dear readers. As the Gulf of Mexico swooshes to and gently recedes from the shore, I remember my own childhood years with my family in Florida and summers spent at Paul's family farm. These memories seem to mark my need to write straightforwardly about grief and its antidote, which is mourning.

For fourteen years, I have been struggling with grief and mourning from personal experiences. I have won my knowledge the hard way—through losses both expected and shocking. I hope that you will benefit from what my experiences have taught me, and I hope that you will find relief from your own grief as I have found some peace with mine. Mourning is hard work, but work worth doing.

Death in a Family

On a July day in 2000, when deep blue skies spoke of summer, my older brother George, an experienced small aircraft pilot, was killed in an ultralight plane crash. The plane went down with George and another experienced pilot just short of York Airport in Pennsylvania. He was forty-four, enthusiastic about life, just beginning a new business that I knew far too little about, and happily raising three children with his beloved wife of twenty years. George loved technology, and it seems like every day that I see new technological products, games, and communication tools reminding me he isn't here to enjoy them. In the mid-1980s, with the wonder of a child, he showed me *Dragon Slayer II, Xanadu*, one of the earliest action role-player video games. "Wow! Look how the computer game adapts to the player and does what I want it to do!" He told me, "The future holds untold possibilities." Those possibilities are coming to fruition daily, and I miss that George can't enjoy them. So does his family, of course, as they have struggled with life without him.

Fifteen months after George's death, in October 2001, my paternal grandmother, who had suffered Alzheimer's for many years, finally succumbed to old age. She was in her nineties and had been a very healthy woman, so the brain devastation had years to work on her mind while her body refused to quit. In the end, she had only stories to tell of a childhood in Hungary and fear of marauding soldiers—when she spoke at all. On the heartbreaking day when my father told Grandmom about George's death, she didn't even recognize Dad as her own son. When Grandmom died, we grieved, but felt relief as well. My father, however, obviously felt devastating grief regarding both his son and his mother. He had been hit all too hard.

Two months later, in December 2001, my father—merely sixty-six—died of a violent heart attack in his sleep. Dad was the senior George, and he worked as most parents of baby boomers did: hard, focused, endlessly. With two partners, Dad created an engineering business that made a genuine difference in dozens of people's lives—not only from the work they did so well, but from the jobs that enabled the employees to feed and clothe their families. The business fed and clothed my family, too, but it often pulled Dad from us as he strived for its success. My father was a charming man that people loved. Dad died of heart failure, although I believe that his broken heart over George's death sealed his fate. Dad seemed defenseless against depression, anxiety, and grief, exacerbated by years of hard work, a reliance on alcohol, and worries about his retirement years due to post-Enron losses. At that point, I think my father didn't have a chance. Neither, then, did my mother as she shouldered the dual losses of her first-born child and her husband over whom the sun rose and set.

In the summer after my father died, my mother-in-law Kitty also breathed her last. She had suffered cruelly from a double neurological whammy of Alzheimer's and Parkinson's diseases. A vibrant, active senior who loved to walk, bowl, and do aqua exercises, Kitty was reduced to repeating whatever was said to her and curling into a fetal position. Although deeply saddened, we were relieved at Kitty's death because her suffering was over.

There are consequences after any death, often described as a ripple effect. A stone tossed into a pond causes a series of ripples to emanate from the center of the water. As the water swells, moving ever outward, it connects with other objects in the water, touching them and changing where they sit in the water. Their new position then causes changes to other objects as the water moves around them.

Ripple effect of grief

Similarly, every death has ripple effects on those who are connected to the deceased. Bereaved people's grief and mourning behaviors touch family, friends, and co-workers, and even strangers to the event. No one grieves alone in the sense that anyone in our social sphere can be affected by our grief. Not only can other people be affected, however, but our own health and ability to confront other stressors can be affected by death's ripples.

Perhaps, then, it shouldn't have been a surprise that only three years after George's death, my mother Daryl was diagnosed with non-Hodgkin's Lymphoma. Although I had a younger brother and sister, Mom's care fell primarily to me as the oldest child and the one in closest proximity. Together, Mom and I went to chemo sessions, and I visited almost daily from a twenty-mile distance throughout the procedures and chemo treatments. We cried and laughed together, and we tried to figure out the changes in our family since death had begun to visit. Mom passed her chemo phase, but she nearly died the day that the doctor told her she was in remission. That morning, her right leg had thrown clots into both lungs and almost killed her before the situation was brought under control eight frightening days later. I was stunned into unthinking, robotic-like actions. Since then, thankfully, Mom's cancer has not returned, but we believe that the cancer was connected to her intense grief.

Years passed, seemingly quiet, and life got easier on most counts. However, a fever was raging in our family, and we found ways to pretend it was not going to be catastrophic. My youngest sibling Kathy, deeply bereaved, had fallen apart after George died and broken further after Dad's death. She never really recovered from either, in part because she hid her grief. Kathy tried to conceal from all but her husband and two teenage children that she was spiraling downward and becoming ever more depressed and mentally ill, as well as more reliant on alcohol to suppress her pain. Around 2007, she cut off contact with her extended family. By April 2010, she lay dying in a Pennsylvania nursing home, suffering from cirrhosis at age forty-seven, having let go after years of pain, trauma, and deadly sadness. Kathy passed away quietly and with dignity, but she left a swath of devastation that has rocked our world.

While I think the metaphor of rippling water generally is apt, I have to say that rather than a ripple, Kathy's death has affected me more like a tsunami. Grief tinged with guilt and anger has crashed against forgiveness and the deepest humility I have ever experienced. My husband Paul and I took in our nephew, Kathy's son, to get necessary medical care for him and to provide him with some of the life basics necessary to launch a young adult into today's world. Our niece—resilient and fiercely independent—and my brother-in-law also have come to share some of their lives with us as we all pick up the pieces.

Most recently, we have experienced more grief as we said goodbye to Paul's father in 2011, an eighty-eight year old whose tired heart was functioning at twenty percent toward the very end. Paul Sr. died the most peacefully of all—also in his sleep but without the active grief and fears for the future that my father had experienced. In June of that year, my spiritual director, Dom John Farrelly of St. Anselm's Abbey, died of pulmonary fibrosis.

All told, it has been a tumultuous fourteen years, and I have no illusions about the future. My family simply is in the season of life where more of us will die and we will need to integrate those deaths into our lives. I share these events so that you can know that I understand grief—and some of what you may be feeling—from experience.

Responding to Death

Beyond personal experience, though, I felt a call to learn more about helping others and myself through grief. I have earned a certification in Compassionate Bereavement Care from the MISS Foundation, a Death and Grief Studies Certificate from the Center for Loss and Life Transition in Fort Collins, CO, worked as a Facilitator-Trainer for the National Catholic Ministry to the Bereaved (NCMB), and am affiliated with GriefWork for the Servants of Mary. Since 2004, I have facilitated grief support groups, workshops, seminars, and retreats. For the past five years, I have trained other bereavement facilitators, and my mother and I co-facilitate a Bereaved Parents of the USA (BP USA) support group in Harford County, Maryland. I also am the author of *Good Words: Memorializing Through a Eulogy*, six derivative booklets (*Good Words: Eulogies for Children, Good Words: Eulogies and Children's Voices, Good Words: Nontraditional Eulogies, Good Words: Eulogies and Religious Settings, Good Words: Eulogies and Difficult Situations, and Good Words: Writing and Delivering a Eulogy)*, and co-author of *More Good Words: Grief in the Workplace*. All of these books have been developed to help people find the words and actions to remember their loved ones.

It was in training with Dr. Alan Wolfelt, a noted author and grief counselor, that I first heard of a difference between *grief* and *mourning*. Until then, I had perceived of these words as synonymous. However, they are, indeed, different in meaning, and each word indicates a different response to death or other significant losses.

Grief is an internalized, emotional response that happens—normally, naturally, and necessarily—upon learning of a loved one's death or accompanying another significant loss. Mourning, however, is an externalized response to the grief that we can choose to engage or to forgo. Mourning uses the emotions that we may feel somewhat passively with grief. Intentional mourning is both active and powerful, and it leads to hope and healing.

Choosing mourning is the healthiest response to death that we can have. Unfortunately, our North American society does not encourage active mourning, and the bereaved get mixed messages: *I'm sorry for your loss. You must feel awful. By the way, when do you think you'll be ready to get back into the swing of things? We miss you at the gym.* Such messages can be painfully depressing to those who are grieving a loved one and struggling with the need to get through each day.

This book is about engaging grief through mourning. It's about *doing something with the pain of grief* that, over time, helps it to dissipate. In doing and performing acts of mourning, we learn to integrate grief into our lives. We figure out how to embrace the grief and carry it in ever-decreasing weights until we begin to understand that to grieve is to be fully human because we have loved and can still love.

Images of Grief

In this book, I use a number of images to convey my understanding of grief and mourning. First, the cover of this book uses the image of the butterfly at Jerusalem's Wailing Wall. The Wailing Wall is a place to emote to God about grief and other pain. Wailing is a mourning sound—much like that of a wounded animal—that many cannot give themselves permission to make. The butterfly begins life as a caterpillar, seals itself into a cocoon, and emerges with gorgeous wings that give it an entirely new world into which it flies. Like the dragonfly images on the cover of *Good Words: Memorializing Through a Eulogy*, the butterfly represents rebirth. When these rebirth symbols are found at the Wailing Wall, we can understand that our grief in loss is intimately connected with rebirth—both our own and that of our deceased loved ones.

As I am writing this book on a retreat at the Gulf of Mexico, I find myself walking frequently on the shore. Three more images come from my walks, and they permeate this book. One is the rushing and receding of water upon the shore. Another is found in the spiral shapes that form many seashells. A third image also involves seashells.

Spiral nature of a shell

I happened upon a *carrier shell* on the beach. Carrier shells house sea snails. As the shells grow, they cement objects to their outside rim—pebbles, smaller seashells—whatever the snail finds. Marine biologists are not certain whether these objects serve as camouflage or ballast that keeps the snail shell from sinking into the sand. Either way, the carrier shell is no longer just the shell that houses the snail; it now permanently carries other objects as the snail moves about. This particular type of shell does not integrate the objects *into* its own shell; rather it *carries them on its shell* wherever the snail goes.

Think of this carrier shell as toting along the grief of our lives. Over the years that the original snail or other sea creatures use this living shell, it continues to take on the weight of new objects, new grief. Over time, the shell becomes old and stops growing, yet it remains encrusted with the grief objects forever. The image of the carrier shell is not a positive image for our grief because the objects—our grief—are continually carried, but never integrated into the shell's life.

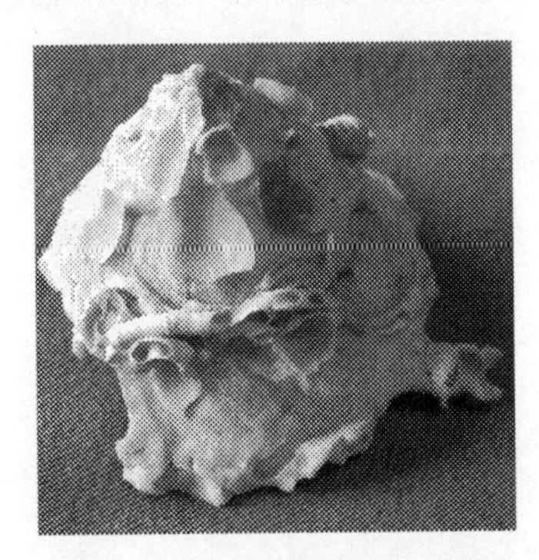

Carrier shell

I also found several small rock-like objects on the beach. Within the rocks, pocked with apparent air holes, are tiny seashells. These shells both grew *onto* and *into* the rock over years of tumbling in the sea. Through an oddly beautiful cementing process, these rocks both contain and are made of the shells. I'll call them "shell stones" here.

Shell stone

These shell stones are like another sea creation indigenous to Florida waters: coquina (Spanish for "small shells"). Coquina is a sort of stone made of tiny seashells that have bonded together over many years. They literally are formed from *layer upon layer of shells* that masons can cut and dry for building. The Castillo de San Marcos, a fort at St. Augustine, Florida, was built from coquina because the seashells—while terribly fragile in their individual state—are amazingly strong and resilient in their bonded state. Although technically still shells, they also are stone. The Castillo de San Marcos was able to withstand several bombardments from attacking ships because the coquina absorbed the impact of cannonballs while different kinds of stone would have shattered.

Coguina

Imagine the coquina and the shell stones—both of which take shells into themselves—as a life that integrates grief. Rather than carrying it around forever as grief cemented to their bodies (and hearts), these rocks absorb the grief and make it a part of their very nature. Indeed, as coquina shows, they become strong because of the grief shells. If, like these shells, we change ourselves by having embraced and integrated grief into our lives, then we can open our hearts to loving and embracing others, which ultimately changes us.

I use these carrier shell, shell stone, and coquina images as metaphors for grief and mourning in this book. Think of grief as a seashell—natural to life, yet fragile to carry without breaking your heart further. The temptation is to cast off this grief (shell), as it's not what we want in our lives. Yet, we cannot cast off grief because it has been cemented mysteriously to us and it has become a part of us. If we cannot cast it off, maybe we can pretend that it isn't there. But, pretending does not really work either. The grief is stuck to us like it is to the carrier shell, and it is visible to everyone in our lives. Therefore, the work of grief and mourning is not to cast it off, to wear it on the outside, or to "get over" it. The work must be to find ways to integrate the grief (shell) into our lives. If we can accept the grief as part of us and, embracing it, allow it to grow into our broken hearts, then we can take the good that it can provide. Shell stone and coquina provide structural strength to withstand bombardments; integrated grief provides similar structural strength for the hurts of life.

In any case, the grief shell becomes a part of us. If geologists were to take apart the carrier shell, coquina, or shell stones, they would find the history of the shells—their age and their experiences of where they formed in the sea. If historians were to probe us, the bereaved, our grief shells also would tell a story of who we are, who we have grieved, how we have or haven't integrated that event into our lives, and whether we have used that grief for better or worse in our lives and the lives of others. Our experience and understanding of past events influence how we live today and in the future.

Our grief is part of our history. Like scars on the skin, we can try to erase our experiences with loss in a vain attempt to "get over" it. No. Grief does not need to be erased. We benefit greatly by acknowledging and honoring our grief. We learn from being honest and authentic with it. Grief is a natural, normal, and necessary part of life. Grief can enrich us emotionally and spiritually because It's as much a part of the relationship we have shared with the deceased as the passion with which we have loved that person. Grief can be used for knowledge, wisdom, and strength. Thus, it's helpful to befriend grief and work with it through mourning activities. That is the major message of this book.

Please use this book as an opportunity to mourn actively. Let it help you to give yourself full permission to mourn as actively and passionately as you have loved. *More Good Words: Practical Activities for Mourning* provides a broad range of mourning activities designed to stimulate your own ideas for mourning in ways that make sense to you, your family, and those people who grieve with you.

Part 1

Grief and Mourning

Grief is an emotionally internal and somewhat passive set of feelings experienced by most people upon the death of a loved one. Mourning is an emotionally external and active response to that grief. Both grief and mourning are normal, natural, and necessary; however, while we recognize grief after most losses, we often don't understand the need for actively mourning those losses. In part, this problem comes from a contemporary North American cultural tendency to deny the reality of death and its impact on us.

When we consciously recognize the need for mourning and apply some practical actions to grief, we open up hope and, as Dr. Wolfelt says, set an intention to heal.

This section of the book is written to help you understand the various faces of grief and the necessity of mourning. It also attempts to assure you that you aren't helpless in encountering grief. In fact, you can take back control over the powers of grief through mourning.

Chapter 1

The Power of Grief

> Grief is like a wound that needs care to heal, and it always leaves a scar. It is like an assault—grief hits fast and leaves us feeling violated and vulnerable. Grief sucks. It sucks the breath right out of us, and—if left unattended—it can suck the life out of us too. It feels like a sucker punch to the gut. The blow of grief undoes the world and creates a new reality where safety, security, and certainty no longer exist.

Love and Grief

Love is one of the most powerful forces in human life. I believe that we were created for the express purpose of loving. We bend and sway with the force of love, and we yield to it, giving the beloved much of our energy and attention. We try to give our best selves to those whom we love. Without love, humans simply are not whole, and they don't experience their most crucial emotions. Love is central to our lives.

Standing right beside love and ready to jump into the fray, however, is the capacity to grieve what we have loved and lost. When a beloved person dies or is lost in another way grief can step in unbidden. And yet, grief is as natural, normal, and necessary as breathing air. We are helpless to its initial impact, because grief is the emotional by-product of lost love. It's completely unavoidable when we have given ourselves to love. Without grief, many people who have loved cannot be whole, and they cannot experience their full range of emotions. Undeniably, we humans have both the capacity and the need to grieve just as fully as we have loved.

Grief occurs in the seconds after the phone call or knock at the door that tells us that life will never be quite the same again. Grief sneaks into our consciousness and becomes a curtain separating pre-grief life from grief-filled life. One minute, the world is fine; the next minute, the world has changed reducing us to our primal selves. As the Cheyenne Native American might say, "Our hearts are on the ground."

The space between the *before* and the *after*—the space occupied by the curtain that is falling on our old lives—is a *liminal space*. It's a threshold that we cross, marking a passage between the old, familiar way of life and the new, unfamiliar life of loss. In this liminal space, there's a brief, ethereal moment of the unreal ("This can't be happening!") that occurs before a new reality comes to exist.

What significant emotional events have influenced your life with a distinct *before* and *after*? Was the curtain a public tragedy like:

- The assassination of President Kennedy? (Or Bobby Kennedy, Martin Luther King Jr., or John Lennon?)
- The Challenger or Columbia space shuttle explosion?
- Princess Diana's or Pope John Paul II's death?
- The terrorist attacks of September 11, 2001?
- The school shootings at Columbine, Virginia Tech, or Sandy Hook Elementary School?

This book is about what we can do with the pain of the new reality. For if we don't confront our grief—feel it, move into it, experience it, taste and see it, and eventually let it go—that grief may suck us into a mud so thick that we can scarcely tread before being engulfed, swallowed up, and drowned.

Grief is pain that passively happens. It hits and hurts without warning or permission. Someone we love dies, is killed, passes away, or takes her own life. Someone we love never had a chance or wouldn't take a chance. Someone we love disappears from our presence through a divorce, breakup, or geographical or physical move. When these things happen, grief moves in.

> You were here. Now you're not.
> Grief is here instead.

Grief alters our sense of existence and our sense of self. We're no longer seeing ourselves the same way. It doesn't matter that what we were wasn't ideal. We want it back!

Types of Grief

Below are seven types of loss in no particular order. Each type of loss causes us to grieve. Sometimes, we won't even be sure what we're grieving. However, the death of any of these people influences us emotionally.

- **Loss of parent:** *Before my parents died, I was their child. Even though I'm an adult, I liked knowing that Dad ruffled my hair while calling me his kitten and that Mom wanted me to eat well, exercise, and have a job that I love. Now they're gone. I feel like an orphan.*

  We tend to expect our parents to die before us—not now but in the parents' later years. Funny how those "later" years become further away in our minds over time. By the time we reach our fifties and our parents are in their seventies or older, we still expect they'll have a good ten to fifteen years of life left. In reality, we dread the loss of our parents, perhaps believing that when the people who joined their lives to give us life have died, we truly are on our own.
- **Loss of child:** *Before my son's death, I trusted that my children would be okay. I would die first in the proper, natural order of things. Since he died, I worry all the time about my remaining children, their spouses, and their children. There isn't enough time in the day or energy in my bones for all of this sadness.*

The loss of a child is never expected and is completely against the natural order of things. We believe children should not die before their parents. Those who have lost a child will say that it's the most devastating loss. In this book, I won't compare types of loss to say which is worse. All losses are different. However, there is something especially tragic, heartrending, and haunting when a child dies. Parents lose the hopes and promise of a life to be lived, and no one and nothing can replace their child. Sometimes, only other bereaved parents truly can understand what these parents experience and feel.

- **Loss of spouse or significant other:** *My wife died. I used to know who I was in the world. Since she died, I don't know who I am anymore. Am I still a husband? Does she still love me? Will anyone ever miss me like I miss her? What do I need to do to see her again?*

  Loss of spouse or significant other can happen to anyone. Those who are widowed face a loneliness that they had not suspected would come about—often because they were married so long that they learned how to operate as a couple and forgot some of the nuances of being single. Especially in successful marriages, spouses will say that they chose their mates and made promises to stay together "until death do us part." They grieve precisely because they kept that promise. The problem is that death was not supposed to happen to the deceased but to the survivor. We rarely think that we will be the one left alive, alone and scared. Whether one is legally married or not makes no difference in terms of grief. Losing a significant other can feel like losing a spouse, yet it may not be validated as such by relatives and friends.

- **Loss of sibling:** *Until my brother died, I was the second child. After he died, I became the oldest and my parents' caregiver child—unprepared and alone in the task. Sometimes, I get mad at him for leaving me like this.*

  All too often, grief literature fails to discuss the repercussions of losing a sibling. Experience tells me that to lose a sibling is to lose a faithful friend and/or "enemy" who might argue us to the ground but who would fight for us against any outsider.

Siblings are our first taste of peer friendship, and we will always have some kind of connection to them. They are our blood contemporaries. Like the message of a canary in the mineshaft, we know that if death can grab a sibling, it can grab us too. Any myth of dying in "old age," whatever that age might be, is destroyed by the death of a sibling.

- **Loss of friend:** *Before my best friend died, I knew who to call at night to tell my sorrows to or to giggle about the goofs in life with. How can I ever laugh again without her? Who can I tell my secrets to? Nobody understands how I feel.*

  The death of a genuine friend hurts in unique ways. When a friend is someone with whom we share our heart's secrets and whose soul seems to complete our own, then the loss can be as devastating as losing a spouse through death or divorce. A friend can help us to understand a spouse or provide guidance in times of trouble differently from a spouse or significant other. Friend loss, like that of a sibling, often is brushed aside as a lesser loss. We should be wary of any implicit assumption that a friend is replaceable. Although we can love again, no one is replaceable.

- **Loss of co-worker or acquaintance:** *He seemed fine in the office on Friday—joking with us, working, and taking a long lunch. He made sure he said hello to everyone. Was he really saying goodbye? I can't believe he's gone.*

  The loss of someone on the periphery of one's life, such as an acquaintance or co-worker, can remind of us of our own mortality. If a childhood friend or school buddy dies, as with a sibling, we are faced with the inevitability of our own approaching deaths. Similarly, when someone is peripheral to our daily lives, it might seem odd to the outsider that we grieve that person's death. Yet, every person we know or work with resides somewhere in our consciousness. The sense of connection may be mild, but it applies to those we like or certainly respect but know too little about to call a friend. Such a loss in our personal sphere shows the place this person had in our lives by the size of the hole they leave in us.

- **Loss of someone we dislike:** *I just couldn't wrap my head around that woman—she was rude and didn't care about anyone but herself. We'll all be better off without her. In fact, I won't even think about her anymore.*

  It can be surprising how much grief emerges when someone we dislike dies. That person could have been rude, have hurt us deeply in the past, or simply have values or lifestyle practices that turn us off. The reality is that if we dislike—or even hate—someone, we have an emotional investment in that person. Any kind of emotional investment or attachment means that there's a place for the person in our lives and without them filling that space, grief can move in. The only people for whom there can be no grief at all are those from whom we're completely detached. For these people, we carry no awareness. These would include people we don't know as well as those of whom we have let go completely.

Another type of grief involves grieving for someone you didn't know. Even though you may not have known the person personally, you can feel the loss from their death

> One of my friends deeply grieved—with tears and depression—the death of Princess Diana in 1997. She watched the funeral coverage, riveted to the television. My friend didn't know the Princess, of course, but something about Diana's death hit her in a vulnerable part of her psyche. In her case, the fact that the Princess left two young sons behind recalled her own trauma around her father, who died when she was merely five. Her grief was borrowed from the Princess' family, allowing her again to mourn her fatherless life.
>
> My father bitterly grieved the people lost when terrorists attacked and leveled the World Trade Center buildings in New York on September 11, 2001. He didn't know any of those people, but he knew that their parents and children were in terrible pain. As a bereaved parent, he connected emotionally with their loss as another way to comprehend his own grief for George. His grief for other parents was carried over from his grief about George, both enlarging his compassion and his pain.

I was in first grade when John F. Kennedy was assassinated. All the elementary school teachers I saw that afternoon were crying. For what did they grieve? The widow with two children? The country with shattered dreams? Their own fathers, brothers, or friends? The national grief united people who otherwise might have kept their shock and sorrow to themselves.

People I know cried at Martin Luther King, Jr.'s and musician John Lennon's untimely deaths. Some lament lost social change-agents like Pope John Paul II, Nelson Mandela, and Mother Teresa, while others miss Poet Laureate Maya Angelou and celebrities like Elvis Presley and Patrick Swayze. These are all well-known cultural figures that represent a talent, era, or ideal that, once lost, cannot be brought back.

> Grief can surprise us with its ferocity and its depth, and it can do so at the most unexpected of times.

It's important to acknowledge, too, that people grieve the losses of their pet dogs, cats, horses, mice, snakes, and fish. They grieve the loss of health, a job or career, a home they have enjoyed for years, and the stability of a country road that now is a highway. People grieve from divorce, custody battles, the news of an extinct species, the death of a 200-year-old tree, and even the destruction of such cultural artifacts as the twin Buddhas of Bamiyan. While this book is not especially about those kinds of losses, many of the ideas expressed here can help with understanding and working with them.

There are times when a well-loved person dies and our grief is not devastating. Sometimes, that is because the death is a release from tortuous pain, and the caregiving survivor is grateful for that loved one's release. Other times, loss may not be devastating because the bereaved has achieved some level of peace around the death. Such peace typically can't be planned; it happens because of a series of circumstances that often involve great love and forgiveness. If someone close to you dies and you don't experience devastating grief, please don't worry. It's not that your love is faulty. It's that we experience different deaths from perspectives that are grounded deeply in our relationships and beings. Similarly, if someone dies and you feel relief instead of sadness, that also isn't a sign of a faulty love or relationship. Grief hits us in unexpected ways.

Put simply, humans typically grieve loss. The greater the loss, the more we grieve. Additionally, the more unresolved the loss, the higher the likelihood that something unrelated to it can lead to additional grief in the future or trigger an explosive *grief burst*, as Dr. Wolfelt calls it.

A grief burst is a sudden and overwhelming sense of grief and display of emotion—like being at the race track, seeing the winning horse, and noticing that the jockey's silks are the beloved's favorite color. A grief burst might take the form of crying for no apparent reason at work, in the grocery store, or at the dry cleaners. It can happen in church when a particular hymn is sung or in the car when the radio station goes on a Johnny Cash bender. Sometimes people stop going to familiar places in an effort to stave off disconcerting grief bursts.

Grief Is Natural, Normal, and Necessary

Grief sounds pretty awful, doesn't it? Those of us who have experienced it know that grief is difficult to handle, terrible to feel, frightening to experience, and exhausting at the cellular levels of our bodies. *Nonetheless, I think grief is our friend at those same cellular levels.* As I explained earlier, to grieve means we have loved. Grief fills the hole left by the immediate loss of our beloved one (or ones). Grief isn't the enemy, but how we deal with it—or how we refuse to deal with it—can be seriously detrimental to us. Here's why.

Grief is a natural function of being human. We can't hold onto our loved ones forever in this world. Although contemporary American society doesn't like to accept this fact, our human nature is to be born, to live for however long we're able, and to die. Our bodies—even when cremated—return to organic components capable of enriching the earth. None of us gets out of this world alive, but sometimes we can't imagine that we *really* will die!

Our very nature gives us the opportunity to experience loss with the same fullness of passion that we have experienced love. We can't use self-will and discipline to make ourselves love or to stop loving; it happens without our determination. Similarly, grief can't be willed or disciplined away. It can't be compelled either; we can't make ourselves grieve where that feeling doesn't exist. Love and grief co-exist naturally. It is beyond our powers to pretend that we aren't bereaved or to create something out of nothing.

With love, often there's a time of romance and a squishy-stomach, fluttering-heart newness to the attraction. I have felt such feelings for my husband, newborn son, and other important people in my life. These wonderful feelings can last a long or short time while the love evolves into a mature relationship. Once the relationship matures, the fluttery heart may not flutter quite so much, but the experience of loving someone can grow even stronger and deeper. So it is with grief. It begins with an intensity that may double us over in pain. However, this intense, heart-stabbing level of feeling doesn't last forever because grief, too, evolves as we come into relation with our loss.

Coquina and shell stone

It's true that some people remain in pain with a broken heart, but typically, we won't always feel the grief as intensely as we do at first. The images of coquina and shell stones described in the Introduction model how we can embrace and integrate loss as part of a life history. By accepting and owning grief, we integrate it into ourselves and own it as part of who we are. Grief loses its power over us when it becomes one of many transformative emotions that reflect a fully lived life.

Remember that grief is the proof that we love. Notice I did not say *loved*—no past tense verb here. When a beloved person dies, we *still love* that person. The love remains present, and we need to allow ourselves to keep it as a gift to others and ourselves.

Death ends a life, not a relationship

Grief also is completely normal. I know. It feels abnormal. That abnormality comes about in part because grief brings awkwardly painful feelings that differ so much from the love we feel for the deceased. Nonetheless, grief is normal in the human family. Even people who are relieved when a loved one dies after a debilitating illness experience some grief, sense of loss, or emptiness in their lives.

The idea of *normal* is that we conform to the average, every day, or ordinary experiences that others do. Grief isn't right or wrong—it just exists. There's compelling evidence in the graves of prehistoric people that their loved ones grieved their deaths. The careful placement in a protective grave of fine jewelry, weapons, and adornments indicate that the deceased were loved and would be missed. We know today from such mourning evidence as roadside and online memorials that our loved ones are grieved and deeply missed.

Humans aren't the only ones that grieve. Observation tells us that other animals may be capable of grief. Recent photos in the news showed a herd of elephants gently caressing the body of a dead, three-month-old, baby elephant. The herd and the mother showed distress. In another case, two South African elephant herds traveled twelve hours to visit the home of Lawrence Anthony who had been instrumental in their survival and who had just died. No one knows how they knew their benefactor had died, but they spent two days at his home, seemingly paying respects to him. Orca whales, which stay with their families all their lives, swim frantically and make heartrending sounds upon the death of a baby or family member. Mammals that lose their litters may decline and wither with apparent grief, and some recover from their losses when given substitute babies. I recently saw a striking photograph of a mother tiger whose entire litter had died. Although the loss had left her nearly dead from what the veterinarian described as depression, she lay contented as six piglets wrapped in tiger-striped cloth snuggled and nursed from her. Some animals grieve their mates; scientists know that most swans mate for life (although some will pair up again after a mate's death—much like human widows and widowers). While we have to be careful not to ascribe to animals all the same feelings as humans, it's interesting to consider how many animals grieve as a normal part of their experiences with death.

Grief is necessary. I believe that grief, both natural and normal, is a necessary part of both loving and coming to grips with death and other losses. Grief is nature's way of allowing us to experience bereavement and to heal. Even the smallest of children grieve when they are parted from their parents, beloved blankets, or stuffed animals. Anyone old enough to love is old enough to grieve.

Grief is a healthy response to loss because it enables us to experience and feel how precious the beloved is. An unacknowledged loss may lead to prolonged grief that can hinder our ability to love in the future. Pushing away loss can make us sick. It can lead to unhealthy behaviors that feed the ability to keep pushing that grief away. Such behaviors include numbing our emotions with drugs, alcohol, food, gambling, excessive shopping, and the like.

People also need the time that grief allows to make adjustments in life. As part of a ripple effect, the loss of a spouse, for example, leads to other changes—sense of self, financial options, cooking and housekeeping requirements, and changes that involve living arrangements and relationships. People can't make such changes immediately. While grief can cloud our vision, it also gives us a socially accepted time (at least, it should) to make these adjustments.

For me, grief brought about a wider range of emotions than I could access before my loved ones' deaths. I hadn't had enough time to grieve George before Dad died, and my heart felt shredded. Such depths of grief emerged in sadness, spontaneous and extended crying, grief bursts, sleeplessness, and lack of appetite. It surprised me, then, when I found myself feeling joy sometimes. Rather than staying stuck in grief 24-hours a day, my emotional range broadened to a sense of genuine peace and joy at simple things like taking a walk with my dog. I hadn't realized it before, but I spent most of my life in the low-middle of the emotional range where I tended to feel chronically sad. This range is called dysthymia. The depths of grief broke me out of that emotional rut and gave me the gift of the full range of human emotions—from extreme sadness to exhilarating joy. Like the swing of a pendulum, the broad arc swing into grief also meant receiving a broad arc swing in the other direction into joy. For me, grief's gift has been a deeper understanding and acceptance of my human self.

The Many Faces of Grief

People experience grief in many different ways, and it's okay that your experience and mine are different. We're different people with vastly different backgrounds and life experiences. Our relationships with our loved ones also are unique. In fact, it's helpful to understand that everyone's grief is unique. In grief, we're like "snowflakes"—individual, distinctively shaped, and destined to be singular.

The uniqueness of our grief

Even though we're unique, just like snowflakes fall to the same ground, there are common emotions one feels during grief. These emotions are why one bereaved person generally can understand another better than a person who hasn't been bereaved.

One common emotion is a sense of numbness. We may feel numb from shock for days, weeks, or even months afterward, which is nature's way of protecting us from the hugeness of the loss. Imagine the sheer terror and agony of a limb amputation without any anesthetic. The shock and pain alone would knock a person unconscious because the mind typically can't consciously handle such intense feelings. So too with grief, the loss of a beloved person can feel like an amputation. Even when we have been told to expect the death as a part of a terminal illness, our minds can protect and buffer us from the initial realization through the sense of shock. It's in this shock that we can, for a little while at least, deny that death has come. When we use that time to come to grips with reality, shock and numbness can be helpful and healthy.

A number of different emotions may arise in grief, and not all are what we expect of ourselves. For example, we may feel:

- Sadness
- Shock
- Pain
- Anger
- Guilt
- Fear
- Loneliness
- Anxiety
- Relief
- Yearning

It makes sense to feel deep sadness at the death of a loved one, doesn't it? But, I was surprised to find that I also experienced guilt when my brother George died because I hadn't known him as I thought I should. I didn't know he had left his previous job and was starting a flight school business. This lack of knowledge made me realize that we weren't as close as we could have been, and my guilt revealed that I took some responsibility for that distance. Similarly, I felt a deep yearning when my father died because I hadn't said goodbye. I had called my mom and dad the day before he died, but he wasn't feeling well and was napping. I didn't call back that evening because I was Christmas shopping. In the end, I felt guilty having missed the opportunity to speak to him one last time.

Many widows and widowers feel deep loneliness without their spouses and are surprised how anxious they feel about accomplishing the tasks ahead of them. In such cases, these bereaved people also may feel guilt for resenting their spouses for dying without them. My mother struggled for years with deep anger at my father for dying in bed beside her and not waking her to help him. She thought: *How could he leave that way and not say goodbye?* If the spouse had been sick for months or years, sometimes the remaining spouse will express a sense of relief for death to have arrived—and immediately after a sense of guilt for having been relieved.

As we can see, emotional responses to death are complicated and tangled. They're related to our relationships, circumstances of the death, and personalities. It's bad enough that we're bereaved, but we also may question why we feel conflicted and uncomfortable.

These conflicted emotions can lead to many different feelings that erupt in our bodies and minds. We may feel or experience such things as:

- Depression
- Lack of appetite
- Increase in appetite
- Lack of energy or a sense of weariness
- Tightness in the chest or muscles
- Breathlessness
- Headaches
- Stomachaches
- Cognitive confusion and/or absentmindedness
- Sleeplessness
- Inability or lack of desire to get out of bed
- Desire to be left alone socially
- Irritation that others are not including us socially
- Disturbing dreams with or without our loved ones in them

🦋 Uncomfortable anticipation that something else bad will happen

Our desires may conflict with our reality. In grief support groups that I have facilitated, I have heard people wish for dreams of their beloved—ones that reveal the loved one is okay and able to communicate with us. My sister-in-law had one of those reassuring dreams shortly after George died. As she tells the dream, she and the children were in the van getting ready to go on a trip. George was sitting on the porch of their house. She leaned out the car window with one arm resting on the door frame and asked, "Aren't you coming with us?" George shook his head no and said, "I can't. You guys go on ahead. You'll be alright." She told me this dream shortly after his funeral and said that it gave her great comfort because her husband had acknowledged that she was to go through life without him.

Over the years, I have looked for such comfort in my dreams of deceased family, but my dreams typically have not been comforting. For years, if Dad was in the dream at all, he did not look at me or say a word. After having this dream, I physically felt the pain of being ignored by my father and woke up with a cramped belly. Again, for years, when my brother was in the dream, it had the same theme of abandonment. In that dream, he had faked his death—as all his friends now knew—and had a new family and life with a different type of job a few streets away. In the dream, his death was an elaborate ruse to move into this new life without us. Interestingly, no one in the dream except me is mad at him for this deception. I always am disturbed upon waking from this dream, and even now I have the fuzzy sense of needing to do a reality check that George is, indeed, dead and not living around the corner. Because my dreams have shifted over the years and now include concerns about my sister, I see them as a way my mind and heart work out some of my grief.

I share these dreams with you because it's easy to think of ourselves as a little bit crazy in our emotional dealings with grief. In grief support groups and retreats, more people seem comfortable sharing the happy and pleasant dreams. I haven't heard anyone talk willingly about the nightmares. Nevertheless, some people do have nightmares, and these can be a normal part of grieving. Since I know I'm not crazy and that I've been handling my grief in healthy ways, I think it's important for people to know that it's all right to have conflicted feelings about loss. If you've had disturbing dreams, please know that it's normal. They likely will go away, but they may return at special times like birthdays, wedding anniversaries, death dates (or "angel" dates, as my mother likes to call them), and holidays. This, too, is normal and nothing to fear even if we don't like it.

While depression lives in past experiences, anxieties live in the unknowns of the future. Anxiety, therefore, is another challenging emotion to deal with; It's common to worry that something else bad will happen or that we'll will never feel good or right again. People have described this sense to me as worrying that the proverbial "other shoe will drop"—that someone will lose a job or the house will burn down or the dog will run away or that someone else will die. This anxiety can be paralyzing in intensity: it's the anticipation of more sadness and more things we can't control. Anxiety reflects a realistic and normal, though uncomfortable, way to experience an uncertain world after a death.

My mother, who has now lost two of her four children as well as her husband, provides an example of this anxiety. She does not like that I go scuba diving. It took me awhile to figure out why, and her reasoning—unconscious as it may be—makes sense. *Her son fell from the sky and died. Will her daughter go to the bottom of the sea and not come back up?*

When loved ones feel such anxiety, it's kind to provide coping strategies. To help my mom relax about my diving, I showed her a video of me diving in an aquarium. The video helped my mom see how comfortable and happy I was in the water and how well I swim. She seems to feel better about my diving, but I'm still careful to call her when I'm safely ashore.

My husband and son did the same for me after George died. At that time, I would become anxious whenever we were apart. I worried any time they were on the road or if I didn't know where they were. Instead of chiding me for undue fearfulness, they recognized my worry as natural to having just lost my brother to a catastrophic accident. My anxiety eventually faded away. If I worry these days, I'm able to provide my own relief by calling them. Whereas at first I needed them to allay my fears, now I can do that for myself. This ability is "self-soothing," a behavior that increases our independence in a healthy way as we grief.

The Ways We Depict Our Grief

Just as bereaved people tend to feel their grief in unique, we may depict our grief both with common and unique imagery. When I ask people in a seminar or workshop to draw their grief, many draw an object or place toward which one must move forward or upward. Often, there is a path where the bereaved moves forward and then somehow is pushed back or falls down. Typically, there is a vague sense of hopefulness in that a destination is in sight or in mind, but too far away or difficult to reach, revealing a sense of hopelessness and helplessness in the grieving artist.

Falling off the cliff of grief

For example, I've seen a number of drawings of mountains and valleys. In these depictions, people tend to show themselves as being on a path moving up a high mountain. How far along they are on that path depends on how long they've been bereaved. After a summit, there often is some kind of sheer-faced cliff or other drop into a valley. The path may continue from that valley up another mountain as high as the first. Sometimes the next mountain is a bit lower, which seems to indicate variable difficulty or a sense that the next summit *simply must be* lower and easier than the first. The valley sometimes suggests a sense of falling rather than a safe place. In these drawings, the grieving artist may say that there isn't a final peaceful place but only more mountains and valleys, which indicates how grief can block a sense of hope.

Like the theme of mountains and valleys, one bereaved artist depicted a luck-based activity like the children's board game of *Chutes and Ladders*™. In this game, the bereaved moves gradually up a steep ladder and then continues forward on a straight path until she hits a tube where she slides uncontrollably back down. Seemingly, doomed to fate, the bereaved is at the bottom staring up at the steps that she must climb. In this depiction, there also seems to be little hope of reaching the end and winning the game of grief.

The rollercoaster of grief

A similar power-stealing image is that of a roller coaster. Once one is strapped (unwillingly via a beloved person's death) into the coaster, it chugs up a long track, setting the rider up for a gut-wrenching fall to the bottom, where the coaster again picks up speed and terrifies the rider. The only way to end the ride is to get off, which seems impossible to many bereaved people.

Grief is often depicted through water imagery. One type of image involves a lake or river to cross without a boat or waves crashing and receding on the beach. The lake requires one to swim—without any stopping place or floatable objects for rest. Here, the bereaved may have the sense of treading water or of drowning from exhaustion and a distant shore that never gets closer.

The relentless waves of grief

Water also can be presented in the form of ocean waves. Here there is the sense that the bereaved is hit by a wave of grief that pushes and slams him to the ocean floor where he tumbles helplessly in the salt-water sand until the wave gives way. As it recedes, however, that water pulls back forcefully, dragging the bereaved, barely breathing, back into the path of the next wave. This particular picture reminds me of grief bursts except that the griever never gets a chance to recuperate from the emotional burst before another one comes upon him. In this case, the bereaved can't catch his breath and, like the relentlessness of the next coming wave, is constantly at the mercy of unmerciful grief.

It's interesting to me that none of these depictions of grief is linear or a series of set steps to reach the end of grief. Maybe this is because many of us instinctively know that there's no straight-line path to wholeness after a death. Grief specialists agree that the idea of grief as a linear progression from one set of emotions or goals to another is false. Elizabeth Kűbler-Ross, in *On Death and Dying*, popularized the five stages of grief model (denial, anger, bargaining, depression, and acceptance). Kűbler-Ross reported on her observation of 500 *dying* (not bereaved) people who experienced such emotions, which needed to be described and categorized to make sense to readers where were doctors, nurses, and other clinicians. Although she later clarified that the model was not meant to suggest that people must experience these grieving emotions in any order or even at all, this notion of progressive emotions persists.

NOPE: GRIEF IS NOT QUITE LIKE THIS

Denial ⟶ Anger ⟶ Bargaining ⟶ Depression ⟶ Acceptance = End of Grief!

I've heard bereaved people say things like, "I've gotten done with denial, anger, and depression. I guess I still have to go through bargaining before I can accept this death." No. Not at all. Grief is not a straight path to anywhere. A wide range of emotions are involved. Although I see grieving as part of my personal journey on earth, I do not suggest that there is a particular destination to reach. In fact, this view of grief can be harmful rather than helpful. Here's one example.

Recently, one widow I know experienced the first anniversary of her husband's death. She cried with abandon, which was healthy. Yet, she expressed a sense that she had failed because she hadn't reached a "new normal," which is a catchy phrase going around bereavement groups. Sadly, she viewed this "new normal" as a place, a destination she hadn't found. By not experiencing relief at this unknown place, she expressed that all the hard work of grieving she had done that year was worthless. Our group talked about not taking on requirements or goals for grief that don't resonate as a useful understanding of a unique path. The phrases a *new reality* or *new journey* rather than *new normal* seemed more useful to some. Although her pain helped the rest of the group, her sense of failure had hurt her deeply on an already challenging day.

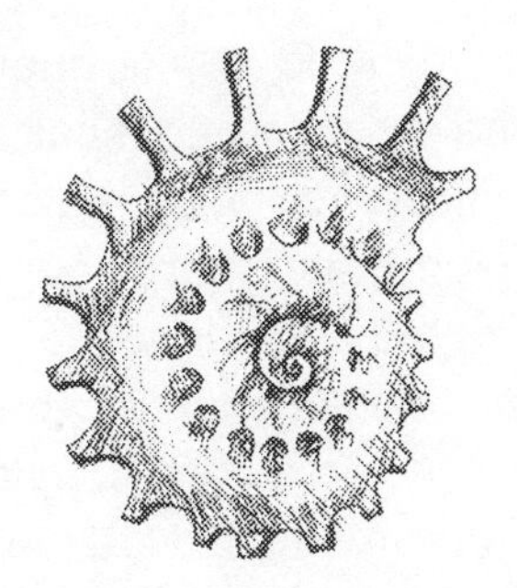

Spiraling grief

Because there is no particular destination or straightforward path through grief, a helpful depiction of grief for me is that of a spiral. A spiral is funnel-like and conical. It's a continuous curve emanating from a beginning point—the curve begins wide and narrows over time to reach a center or tip. Many spirals exist in nature. As these seashell pictures show, the curve circles inward, moving closer to the centermost point.

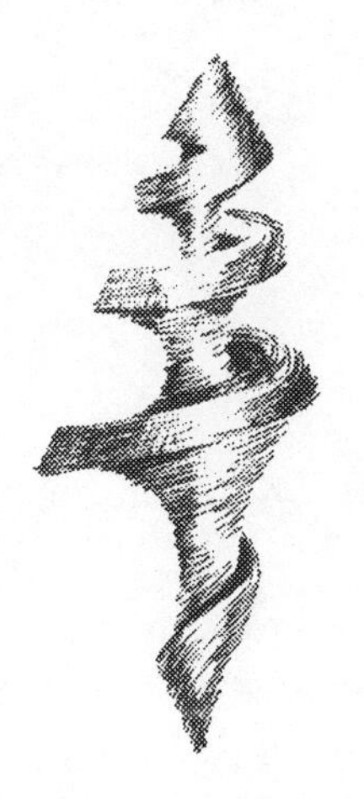

Grief as a journey

Perhaps you're familiar with the spirals that grow within seashells, creating their lovely and intricate shapes. In plants and animals, spirals often are called "whorls." Although there are many kinds of spirals and ways that nature and mathematics depict them, they share a primary characteristic—the curve that revolves around the central point moves more tightly inward in ever-concentric circles that merges to a point.

Let's use the spiral as a way to depict grief. Imagine that early in your grief you experience a sense of despair. Place despair near the beginning point of the conical shell below. Later, you find yourself angry whenever you feel despair. Place that anger on another level of the spiral that corresponds to the original despair. Then, for a while, your emotions tend more to an intense anger—rage—that you can pinpoint above anger on the spiral. As time goes on, place other emotions, like sadness, progressively upward and toward the tip. Of course, you may experience many confusing emotions at once—these are all part of your grief journey.

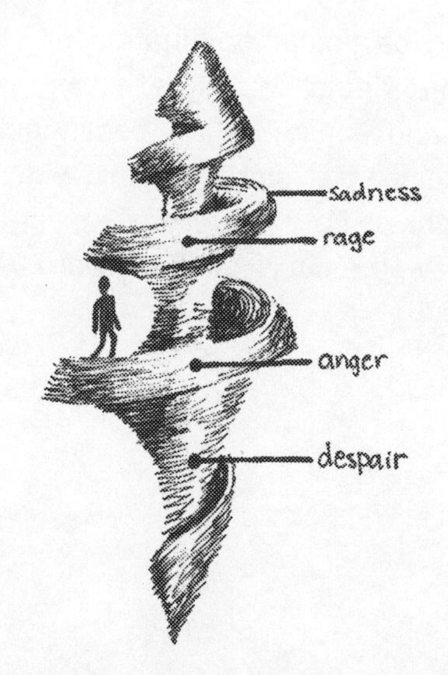

Changing emotions on the grief journey

The spiral of this conical shell reveals that the emotions are related, yet they're notably different because with each emotion you're in a different place—time wise and contextually—in your grief work. By experiencing anger in the sense of rage, the spiral demonstrates that you haven't moved backwards or fallen down in any way, but merely continued on your journey, finding a new experience of a similar emotion.

For me, a spiral or conical image does not carry a sense of failure, helplessness, or hopelessness. There's merely a distance from the beginning point, which represents the original experience of the grief.

Likewise, there's a clear path toward the tip of the spiral, representing my life's journey.

Conflicts and Challenges in Grief

We've discussed the uniqueness of grief, and we've considered that bereaved people share enough similarities to be a community of understanding for each other. We haven't yet talked about some of the ways that people come into conflict about grief. In this conflict, sometimes the ripple effect becomes exceptionally strong, like the tsunami that followed my sister's death. Indeed, the people we most expect to help us and to understand us may be the least able to walk this journey with us. In my experience both as a bereaved individual and as a bereavement facilitator, one of the most challenging aspects of grief is to understand the conflicts that arise in bereaved families. Before we move to chapter 2 and talk about some ways to work with grief, it's important to talk about the challenges that often crop up in families and with others around our grief.

Because this issue of families can be quite complex, I am limiting this section to some of the different ways people might grieve in families. We can then extend these different ways of grieving to close outsiders, including other couples, best or close friends, and co-workers. I'm using my own family system as an example.

There are a lot of books about grief, but too few talk about the challenges of understanding grief in our families. Some of these challenges are normal ripple effects in that what affects me (the mother in our family) will have an impact on my husband and son. For instance, my nephew's need to live with us for three years after my sister's death affected his own nuclear family (they traveled to our house to take him home each weekend, for example), as well as my husband and me (we made space for another person, traveled to many doctor visits, spent more money, and bought and cooked more food, for example). Having another young man in the house even affected our son who does not live with us but who came home for his wedding. He and his fiancé had to stay in the basement room and not in the normal guest room because our nephew was living there with an infected leg. Our son felt cast out of his normal place in the house, which indeed he was. These circumstances were related intimately to my sister's death and illustrate the rippling effect it had on all of us.

Humans are social creatures, and for most of us, our primary social group is family. We have both our family of birth (family of origin) and our nuclear family as adults. In a family of origin—which becomes our extended family when and if we marry—we may have parents, siblings, grandparents, as well as aunts, uncles, and cousins. In our nuclear adult families, we have spouses and our children and later, perhaps, in-laws and grandchildren. Although our grief is unique, we carry expectations about *how our social group will be like us, will grieve like us, and will help us in grief.* We tend to forget that each of our family members also has unique grief about this loss.

Dr. Wolfelt likes to say that grief is a pressure cooker: A grieving person has a high need to be understood and a low capacity to be understanding. Imagine your own family. Each of you likely grieves this loss to different degrees. Yet, each of you has a high need to be understood and a low capacity to be understanding of others. You might find yourselves in a family of people whose grief causes them to be inwardly focused (a necessary part of grief, yes?) and unable to understand—even to want to comprehend—what you are experiencing.

When it comes to grief, everyone experiences it in their own way. One challenge immediately emerges when we believe that our family will grieve like us. Take, for example, the loss of a child. Each parent has lost the child, but each parent will grieve uniquely in part because of their sex and in part because of who they are and how they were raised regarding grief. Sometimes fathers remain more quiet and interior about the loss than mothers, who may want to talk about the child and her death often and deeply. The difference between quiet grief and vocal grief isn't one of degree; it doesn't mean that the mother grieves more than the father does or that her grief is better or more special or anything like that. It simply means that they grieve differently.

However, the bereaved spouses, other children, and extended family may not perceive that difference as merely difference. They may think that the mother is handling her grief "right" and the father isn't or vice versa. Such perceptions may be communicated to the bereaved parents by ripples, making them feel even worse, convinced that something is wrong with one or the both of them. In addition to their grief over the child, they also worry about each other and, in some cases, may criticize each other. Just when their relationship is most crucial to their emotional survival, it may crumble with the pressure of grief perceptions.

Let's look at this same scenario from the perspective of siblings—I have some direct experience here. Traditionally, brothers and sisters had the same mother and father; in contemporary families, there often are stepsiblings, adopted children, and children conceived by fertilization techniques that mask who the biological parents are. In these family contexts, the grief may be more complicated. However, dealing only with the traditional family for simplicity, let us consider the loss of a sibling.

In my family of origin, I was the second child and the first daughter of four children. We were born in the boy-girl-boy-girl order. George and I were born 18 months apart, while our younger brother and Kathy were born 20 months apart with our brother arriving four years after me. We were like two different families with two different sets of parents. My parents were 19 and 20 years old when George was born and in their mid-to-late twenties when Kathy was born. Even though our parents were biologically the same people, they were not the "same people" in that they had matured, become more stable financially, and learned a lot about what to do and not do with their children. George was the baby on whom all practices were tested. Kathy was the baby for whom most worries were suspended. They naturally had very different childhoods and perceptions of the world.

In a similar vein, we all had different perceptions of our parents and of each other. For a simple example, George resented that our parents allowed me to ride my bicycle further from home at a younger age than he had been allowed; but, he was the test baby and his riding skill convinced my parents that it was safe to let me ride further from home. My younger siblings had still more freedom in that area. George sometimes expressed that our parents were harder on him than on anyone else; in a way, they were. One way to understand that "hardness" is that they matured and became more confident in their parenting, which deepened their understanding of their children's capabilities.

Children may not recognize these differences, which can become lifelong irritations. Bigger concerns than who was allowed to ride a bike whatever distance and age can become huge differences of opinion and perceptions among siblings as years go on. Siblings literally may take such slights to their graves unless they make conscious efforts to let them go.

Relationships among siblings differ, too. Age, sex, and place in the family matter. Add to these kinds of issues the fact that siblings have natural connections and disconnections among themselves. I was closer to George in age and we functioned as a pair: "George and Beth, come home!" I could play with him, count on him to watch over me, and know that he would tease me mercilessly. My younger brother and Kathy had a similar pairing. However, Kathy had a special affinity for George that came from being the family's baby. As such, he coddled and cuddled her, calling her loving nicknames until she became about four-years old and he was entering adolescence. As George grew up, he grew beyond her, and she often expressed a sense of abandonment. My younger brother, on the other hand, seemed to me to struggle against George's tendency to tell him (and all of us) how to live our lives "better." As the oldest, George seemed to want to guide his younger siblings into the world, but we wanted to do life our own ways. We clashed about this issue from childhood through adulthood.

When we dissect a family in this way, it becomes obvious that we have no choice but to grieve the deceased sibling differently. I felt as if half of me had been torn away when George died. He and my father were the first men in my life. Because we really can't know someone else's grief, I don't know what my younger brother experienced regarding George when he died. Kathy expressed that she felt abandoned again, and I wonder whether she ever got over that sense of abandonment. That we had different perspectives makes sense because we can only grieve in our unique ways *in relation to the other.* Our relationships with George differed immensely. For our purposes in this book, let us say that *each of us grieved a different brother*—despite the fact that we came from one intact family.

One of the things, then, that makes family grief so complicated is our relationships with the deceased and the living. In caring for our bereaved parents—because that is what many bereaved siblings perceive as their responsibility—my siblings and I had very different. At first, I tried to emulate what I thought they missed in George. When I finally understood that I couldn't replace him, I relaxed into being myself. I think that my younger brother checked in separately with Mom and Dad, particularly trying to engage our father in some new work possibilities that might renew his life. Kathy checked in as the fun person who might provide family activities and comic relief. Our grief practices with our parents, then, also differed according to learned roles and our unique selves.

I share this personal scenario to clarify the complexities of grieving in a family. Many families struggle with each other at just the moments when they most want and need to join and form a tight-knit unit. They get angry with each other, judge and gossip about one another, and fight. The water of grief ripples outward, and they blame each other for not taking on the roles that each thinks is necessary for the other. They may get angry when one family member chooses not to mention the name of the deceased member while that person thinks the others rake up pain by mentioning that name. Our good wishes for each other and strong desires for closeness can be impeded by our unique grief *and* family places.

As such, it's easy to see why some families that typically work well together may find that grief challenges them. When we consider families that are "dysfunctional," more complications emerge. In my observations and talks with the bereaved, it's rare that a family that doesn't communicate well during good times is able to function in emotionally challenging times like bereavement. Throw into the mix a cousin or two, aunt and uncle, and close family friends, and it becomes clear that family grief can lead to many hurt feelings and miscommunications. There are multiple opportunities to hurt each other daily—and just as many opportunities to love each other better if we only know of that need for kindness and understanding.

To help mitigate some of these issues, I strongly urge bereaved family members to talk together frequently. The families that heal the best tend to communicate clearly about their needs. Here are some practical steps to take both before and after a funeral or memorial ceremony:

- Plan a family get-together before the funeral to talk about the different ways you want to memorialize your loved one. This isn't a good time for surprises.
- Decide the best ways to support yourself and your family members.
- If you have a specific desire (to write the eulogy, for example) or a need (such as to be driven to the services), speak up and ask for help. Don't assume that others will automatically know what you need; they're grieving, too.
- If someone in the family has helped you particularly, say thank you. Don't assume that this person will know what you're thinking or feeling.
- If a particular family member tends to turn attention to him or herself during stressful times, make sure that person has a kind friend to watch over his or her needs. This attention will help to cushion the entire family.
- If you typically fight with your siblings or other family members, give yourself a buffer of a thoughtful friend or additional time by yourself. Be especially generous in your response to others to avoid unpleasantness during these stressful times. Try not to perceive a slight in what someone else has said or done.
- Stay away from destabilizing influences like alcohol or recreational drugs. If a family member is inebriated, help him or her if you can do so without becoming upset; otherwise, ask a friend to help.
- Try to eat well, drink enough water, exercise lightly, and get some rest whenever there's downtime. Naps are great during these stressful days.
- Plan a post-funeral meeting (and future meetings) where any legal or other issues can be addressed. Keeping these issues from piling up can be a stress reliever. Many legal and practical actions must be accomplished after a death in the family. Consider shelving the ones that don't have to happen immediately.
- Usually, one person should take charge and everyone else in the family can offer input on decision-making. Keep in mind

the old adage: Too many cooks spoil the stew. Try to get along with the person chosen for the hard work of executing a will or disposing of an estate. Even though that person has "power," a loved one's death is not the way most people want such power.

- Whenever possible, let go of old slights in order to make this time as a family work. In effect, *you are a new family with a different configuration*. New families, like new cars, get scratched and dented. Avoid bringing old wounds to the table because these will magnify the new-family scratches and dents—sometimes creating major fights and irreconcilable family splits.
- You are bereaved. Treat yourself and others with care. Broken hearts need special attention.

I leave this chapter with this thought: We judge each other perhaps too easily and find each other lacking. Fortunately, because we want the best for each other, we can change our approach to be less judgmental and more loving as we deal with our grief in our unique, yet common ways. We can do that by mourning together.

Grief hurts. Mourning helps.

Chapter 2

Mourning Heals Grief's Pain

As we have seen in chapter 1, grief is complicated, unique, and ultimately challenging. It attacks everyone at some point in life, and it steals upon us suddenly, even when a death or other loss is expected. Yet, grief also is a gift. Sorrow is part of being fully human.

Tears of grief

One important idea that we need to consider about grief is that it's internalized emotion that happens without our permission. It comes upon us stealthily or openly, but it comes when we feel the loss of someone or something beloved. Yet, if we try to handle the grief passively—with no action or intention on our parts—we may remain in grief for a long time. Moreover, the grief will negatively influence our ability to feel joy and to live and love well.

We need to address the grief by mourning. Mourning externalizes grief and makes it available socially—within the family and other circles. It's an active approach to the feelings that grief passively gives us. It involves ceremonies and activities that take infinite shapes. Most importantly, it involves doing things that help us to confront the pain head on. Mourning allows us to walk the journey of grief and to be enriched by it.

The need for active mourning comes at a time when many of us are least compelled to do anything because grief saps our energy. We can take our time with mourning, and we can do it a little at a time. We can mourn over periods of time that suit our own needs. But mourn we must. The hard work of mourning eventually leads us to peace with our losses, acceptance of its reality, and integration of the loss in our lives.

The Work of Mourning

As an active response to grief, mourning is hard work. Dr. Wolfelt's has put together a list of six needs of mourning.[1] Below, I explain these six needs to help us talk about what mourning looks like and why it can be hard—but necessary—for us to do.

1. **Accept the reality of the death.**

   We must face the fact that our loved one no longer is alive and cannot participate in our daily lives. This requires breaking through any denial that we have regarding our loved one's death. Such denial doesn't include dreams. For example, my dreams of abandonment by my brother and father I presented in chapter 1. These dreams don't mean I don't know my loved

---

[1] Alan Wolfelt, *Understanding Your Grief: Ten Essential Touchstones for Finding Hope and Healing Your Heart* (Ft. Collins, CO: Companion Press, 2004). See also J. W. Worden, *Grief Counseling and Grief Therapy: A Handbook for Mental Health Practitioners.* (New York: Springer Publishing Co., 1982). His four tasks of mourning are to: (1) accept the reality of the loss; (2) experience the pain of grief; (3) adjust to the new environment where the deceased person is missing; and (4) reinvest energy in life, loosen ties to the deceased, and forge a new type of relationship with them based on memory, spirit, and love.

ones are dead. Denial can come out in dreams, but I think true denial is more visceral and powerful than our dreams.

For example, when George died, my sister Kathy participated in the making of funeral plans. She cried when she heard the news and rushed to my parents' sides; she joined our nervous laughter; and she rationally questioned other pilots about what might have happened to make the plane crash. By all appearances, she had accepted George's death. At the funeral home, however, when the family entered to view my brother's body before the public was welcomed, Kathy took one look at the casket and immediately collapsed to the floor. She was unable to breathe. I knelt by Kathy and breathed with her until she could move to a chair; there, we sat breathing and looking into each other's eyes until she was able to say what she needed to say: "Oh, my God. He's dead." Her first mourning task was to accept that George was dead. Only by viewing his body would her heart and soul accept his death. The rest was going through the motions.

This anecdote illustrates one crucial value of a vigil or wake where people can view the body. Years ago, a family would clean and dress the deceased's body in "Sunday" clothes for the funeral. The acts of touching the body and honoring their loved ones by washing and clothing them brought home the reality of death. This ritual has been transferred from the family to the funeral home. The closest task many of us get is to choose the deceased's burial clothes and bring them to the funeral home. A wake and funeral service once was the next most common way to introduce people to the reality of a death. It's a long-held mourning tradition—perhaps the most important one—that begins the formal and public mourning process for the bereaved. For this reason and others, I'm sad when people cannot view their deceased's body or choose to forgo a funeral service.

Experience has taught me that the "reality of the death" typically includes multiple layers of reality. When one is widowed, for example, the remaining spouse must take over the household chores and decisions, some of which are unfamiliar. Each additional task is a reality of the death. When one has experienced the death of a parent who was ill with cancer or any other painful disease, it's necessary to deal with any personal or familial trauma around sickness that may occur from that experience. Any worry about family members becoming similarly ill is a reality of the death. When a grandchild, niece, or nephew must go through life without a parent, their ongoing needs for parenting are realities of the death as are many emotional issues that emerge in the ensuing years. There is, in fact, no single reality of the death to accept but rather a series of consequences—realities that make themselves evident over time. Each of these, if accepted as a reality of the loved one's death, becomes a little easier to bear. Yet each of these is a reality that must be accepted even many years after the death.

2. **Let yourself feel the pain of the loss.**

   There is no doubt that grief is painful, as we discussed in chapter 1. Our bodies and minds often protect us with the feeling of numbness so we don't have to feel all the raw pain at once. Like an amputation without anesthesia, if we feel all that pain, we may lose consciousness or even die. Some people have had heart attacks in response to such grave news as the death of a loved one. As a means of protecting ourselves from dying from a broken heart, our bodies and minds respond with shock and numbness.

   However, we can't stay protected from this pain forever, which is why shock wears off gradually. Dr. Wolfelt suggests that we take our pain in small, manageable bits. He calls this "dosing" our pain. Before we can dose the pain, however, by an act of choice, we must allow that pain to emerge; *we must feel it*. This means not overmedicating that pain with alcohol or drugs unless under a doctor's orders; even then, it may be wise to consult with a second health care professional. It also means walking toward the pain to embrace it as part of our love for the deceased.

   Mourning activities like the funeral or visiting the gravesite to see a headstone or visiting with another widow to share experiences of death all have one thing in common. They are ways to confront the pain actively and purposefully. It's not intuitive to walk toward pain. If someone invites you to take your shoes off and walk on burning coals, it's likely that you will refuse. Who wants burned feet? One widow told me that she and her husband did once walk on red-hot coals as a spiritual exercise and that her grief hurts much worse than the burning coals. So, it's not lightly that I recommend embracing the pain. The idea is that if we move into the pain and confront it head on, it will have less power over us. We will fear the pain less. With less fear, we can find ways to mourn rather than sit passively with the grief. The Sufi poet Rumi once said: *The cure for the pain is the pain.* His words can guide us in our grief.

3. **Remember the person who died.**

   One of the reasons that grief hurts so much is that we fear losing the memory of the person who had died. We worry that we will not recall his voice, how she laughed, or what he looked like at intimate moments. Many people can dispel these fears because they own recording devices like video and still cameras and voice recorders. They may keep the loved one's cell phone with its answering machine message to call and hear, for example. YouTube videos shared online have taken the place of showing old-fashioned home movies, and we can share those images with others forever. These are one kind of memory.

   Electronic devices that offer digital memories are wonderful. However, the day-to-day remembering of this person in our lives involves so much more. One way to deal with grief is to try to forget the deceased ever lived, but this is not a healthy approach. To *always remember* the deceased's life is the better way because it recognizes that this person has been a formative and active part of our histories and that we would not be who we are today without that person. By deliberately remembering our loved one in healthy ways, we integrate this death into our lives as surely as the living person was a part of us. Mourning activities can help us to remember this person.

For example, at his wedding, one nephew lit a special candle and put it in a place of honor for his father. The candleholder was imprinted with an image of my brother George and his infant George, my nephew. For another example, one bereaved parent and his wife remembered their daughter on her birthday by going to a restaurant and placing a photograph of her at her otherwise empty seat. Remembering a loved one doesn't need to be public. It's possible to create a private refuge or shrine in the home for photographs and special objects that link to the deceased—keeping it healthy by not making an entire room or home into a shrine. For another example, one can donate to a charity in the loved one's name.

A memory candle

Perhaps the most simple and difficult—yet most powerful—way to remember a deceased loved one is to say that person's name frequently and to talk about him or her in general conversation. This mourning activity can make other people uncomfortable—people who are not grieving, that is. As bereaved people, we typically want to freely use and hear our loved ones' names. Not to talk about them makes it seem as if they never lived. Some people won't talk about a deceased person because they fear it will remind the bereaved of the death. This is kind, but nonsensical and hurtful. The bereaved never forget that they've lost a family member or friend. They only worry that everyone else has forgotten. It's more upsetting to the bereaved not to hear a loved one's name than to hear it.

4. **Develop a new self-identity.**

Our identities—child, parent, spouse, sibling, friend, lover, co-worker—are tied to some degree to those we know and love. For example, when a spouse dies, the bereaved widow or widower immediately confronts a strange world without the spouse. One widow's bank stopped her from paying for her husband's funeral with their common funds. The explanation was that funds had to be sorted out and that she needed to present a death certificate before drawing on the account. She protested that her name was on the account, but the bank employee insisted that she could not draw on it. The employee went so far as to tell her that she could not write her name as "Mrs. John Smith" anymore because she was no longer married. Obviously, the bank employee handled this case poorly; my friend took her business away from that bank. This absurd story mirrors many of the challenging situations that the newly bereaved confront. People experience crises of identity and ask themselves:

- Am I a wife without a husband?
- Am I a parent without my child?
- Do I have three children or two now?
- Am I the "bread winner" of the family with just a part-time job?
- What is my next step?
- What will I do with the rest of my life?
- Who will take care of Mom and Dad with our sister dead?
- Will my best friend's child still want to see me now that her mother is dead?
- If my mommy is dead, whose little girl will I be?

We often identify ourselves by a role in the family. Bereaved people who have been caregivers to their dying family members may have wrapped months or years into the caregiver's role. Once the individual has died, however, the bereaved caregiver no longer has a set of clearly defined tasks to accomplish each day. That is a loss of role, and the bereaved person must take time to learn what new identity she wants to have. Losing a role means such things as losing the comfort (as well as the stress) of a set time schedule, the warmth of a loved one to snuggle with or hug, and often financial stability.

Developing a satisfying new self-identity requires conscious mourning efforts. Before a new identity can emerge, the old one must be grieved along with the deceased individual. In this case, the reality of death causes the loss of self-identity. Mourning activities that can help with new identities include traveling with a friend to a new geographic location, seeing a career counselor about an interest inventory, and going to a grief support group to share concerns and listen to how other people are reconfiguring their lives. Any of these are deliberate actions that can help to sort out the different roles that we have held and to think about which ones to keep and discard. Sometimes the greatest benefit from these activities is a realization that we can do what is necessary to survive *and* thrive.

5. **Search for new meaning.**

Searching for "new" meaning requires that we first understand the "old" meaning of our lives. To this end, we need to look back at our lives before this death, which is an introspective approach. Our loved ones provide some meaning in our lives. They do that simply by existing. When people marry, for example, they become a couple that has made public promises to each other. They engage in all the activities that their conception of marriage involves. When parents have children, they become more than parents (a role); they learn the meaning of what it is to have children and to be responsible for and to little people until—and even after—they are grown. As children age, their lives take on new meaning as they become more fully part of a family, and eventually they may become both parents themselves and responsible for and to their own parents.

There is another kind of meaning that we tend to look for—meaning of a deeper, spiritual nature. In this case, we ask not what role we play, but why we exist and how our existence is important to others and the world-at-large. In the search for these broader kinds of meaning, we still look at ourselves in relation to others, but we also try to discern our unique gifts. This search for new meaning is "existential" in that it is concerned with our very existence on earth. The devastation of a loved one's death *both* compels us to begin looking for this meaning *and* provides a useful opportunity to do so. This is one of the benefits of bereavement. Because we are still alive and very aware of death, our lives take on a new gravity that can be healthy.

Philosopher Søren Kierkegaard once said: "Life can only be understood backwards; but it must be lived forwards." His words are a reminder that we need to look back at our lives at times, but that we also should live in the present and move into our future. The mourning that we do can help us to search through our pasts for new meanings to apply in our future lives. Sometimes, that meaning is found in a new spirituality and a renewal of faith—within or outside of organized religion. For others, the opposite is true, and new meaning in life cannot be found without first challenging long-held beliefs and potentially casting off certain ones. This process is like a spring cleaning that can enable a newer, deeper spirituality over time.

Another way that people can use mourning activities in search of meaning is quite practical in that they can volunteer the spare time that they otherwise don't know what to do with. They also may look for meaning in the death of their loved one, much like bereaved sister Nancy G. Brinker did when she established the Susan G. Komen foundation to raise funds for breast cancer patients. Such mourning activities provide places to put our energies that grief otherwise absorbs. It's hard work to mourn in such ways, but rewarding for some bereaved individuals and the lives they touch.

6. **Let others help you—now and always.**

We know that grief is painful and unique to each individual. We also know that our suffering is common in various ways that allow us to talk actively with others. We grieve because we've loved. We love in relation to family, significant others, friends, and a greater humanity. As social beings who need love, touch, and communication with other people, it just makes sense to go about our mourning in relation to others. Immediately after a death, having a wake and/or funeral, sitting Shiva, or attending other ceremonies gives us this sense of community in sorrow. After the first days and weeks of the loss, however, it isn't as easy to find that sense of relation with others, and to do so takes conscious mourning efforts.

People often flock to a bereaved person upon hearing of a death. Sending cards, flowers, money to a designated charity, or simply calling or providing food feels good to fellow grievers. These are acts of hospitality—of sharing—that are important to all of the bereaved. For many people outside the immediate family, offering to help is one of their mourning activities, and providing that help enables them to deal with their grief sooner and more fully. We should welcome those offers of help for the sake of those who need to do something for us—that is an act of generosity on our part. Not surprisingly, other tasks will emerge that we can allow people to do for us: mowing the lawn, tending the garden, getting the car

Flowers in memory of a loved one

serviced, and helping with family members. When our energy is the lowest, we need to let others help us.

Sometimes, though, after the bustle of the funeral, the helpers move back into their own lives and we find ourselves alone with our grief. People may say: *I don't remember anything of the funeral or who was there. But, I know people went and I'm glad we did it. Now, though, no one calls. I'm so lonely and I can't stop crying.* It's very sad when people feel forced to go through the challenges of grief and mourning alone. To ease this difficulty, I think it's important to initiate contact with friends who seem to have dropped away. They likely are uncomfortable with our grief and unsure of how to help. Tell your family and friends specifically what you need—a listening ear, food, lawn mowing, a movie companion—and they probably will meet that need. There's no value in making people guess what you need.

Remember: *we grieve because we love in relation to someone.* Therefore, often we can mourn best in relation to others. We heal as we emerge from the cocoon of early grief and return to the society of fellow human beings.

I encourage the bereaved to attend grief support groups when they're ready and if they believe it will help (see chapter 7). Not everyone will do well in a group setting, but many people will; it can be helpful to try out a group or two. Whether the support group is ongoing or for a limited number of weeks, being with other bereaved people allows us to share our memories and tell our stories—as often as we need and to people who can listen. People in a well-run support group can be very generous with their listening because they know that when it's their turn, others will listen to them. We need to tell our stories of love and grief—the illness, the tragedy, the accident, the death—to make these stories more clear, to absorb them, and to let go of what isn't helpful. To integrate the death into our lives, we often need to talk out the details of what happened. If a support group isn't available or doesn't feel like a comfortable option, an individual grief therapist or bereavement coach can provide a lifesaving relationship (see chapter 6).

Allowing others to help us and these other needs of mourning do not end within a few months of the death. Mourning can take a long time—more time than we may think it should. That's okay. That's even normal. We can take our time, moving into and out of mourning as our minds and hearts indicate is necessary. We probably didn't form a relationship with our beloved deceased in a few months, and we can't integrate his or her death in a short time either. In fact, the life and death of this person will be with us forever because we continue to love them. Some tasks of mourning go on for a long time after the death. This isn't a bad thing or a failure on our parts. The blessing of having loved causes us to remember our loved ones in both life and death.

Discomfort with Grief and Mourning

Often, we need to mourn our loved ones beyond the time provided by our immediate families, workplace, or culture. When this happens, we may get signals from the world that we are "taking too long," need to "get over it" or "move on," and even "perhaps you're sick." Please remember: *grief is not an illness*, but it can lead to illness if you don't give it proper attention. A healthy way to take care of grief is through active mourning and eventual integration of the loss into your life. If these activities make other people uncomfortable, it's not your problem. It's their problem.

People who show discomfort with our grief and mourning may do so for various reasons. One is that they hold unhelpful cultural views about grief. They may believe, for example, that three-to-six months is enough time to mourn a death—and for some deaths, like that of a distant acquaintance or a barely known co-worker, that might be true. Alternatively, they may think that grief is unhealthy or even unbecoming. Another reason that people show discomfort with our grief and mourning has to do with their own incomplete mourning regarding a loved one. Like the measles, grief can be contagious—our own grief can force other people to examine any grief that is stuck to their own carrier shells and still needs to be mourned. People don't like that need—no one welcomes the return of old grief that demands new attention.

As we get older, in fact, every time we are bereaved, we may experience our various bereavements as increasingly more entangled unless we take apart the deaths we have experienced and mourn them individually.

In such cases of complicated grief, a private grief counselor can be especially helpful.

> Life is the pilgrimage that begins with birth. It's how well we live that journey that counts. A full life is filled with laughter and tears, joys and sorrows. Make no mistake: Death is a waypoint on this journey, and it is not optional.

Contemporary American culture has a love-hate relationship with the concept of death. On the one hand, we seem fascinated by it and pay particular attention to roadside memorials (wondering who died and how), ambulance activity at accident scenes (wondering how it happened and who was hurt), and stories of murder on the news (wondering whether that could happen *here*). In this sense, we love to know what is happening in other's lives and who has died or not. We gossip about crime in our towns, and we thank heaven that it didn't happen to us. Sometimes, we even judge the family involved.

Equally unbalanced is how our entertainment media is full of death talk and death scenes where the human devastation typically goes ignored. How many movies or television shows do you view weekly that involve someone's death? Car chase scenes typically involve many crashes and a hero excitedly winnowing his way through—and hitting—countless vehicles to win the day. However, the devastation left behind in that scene is rarely, if ever, addressed. As anyone who has ever had even a mild collision knows, each car collision leads to a potentially injured or killed person. But, the chase scene isn't about those people; it is about the myopic needs of the good and bad guys. In that sense, and in the sense that our media also tend to ignore the deep grief that comes with death—unless there is an opportunity to exploit it for increased viewing—we hate to know about death.

In other ways, too, our society looks away from death and grief just when we need to look at them squarely. For example, many funeral homes and mortuaries now advertise their services as ways to "celebrate" the lives of our loved ones. While I agree that a life well lived deserves some celebration, it is premature for most bereaved people to be told they need to celebrate before they have had the chance to grieve. Yet, that is the implicit and backwards message of such advertising. Even though many of us go through the funeral and memorial ceremonies somewhat in shock, we remain aware of the importance of seeing our loved ones to say farewell. For another example, many bereaved workers in our country receive only three-to-five paid days off work—if that—upon the death of a loved one. This time is barely enough to arrange to bury or memorialize the deceased, let alone to grieve.

Before the mid-twentieth century, it was more common to see people observing the need to grieve. People in mourning often identified themselves by wearing black, "mourning" clothes or armbands. They placed black wreathes on the door and stopped their clocks as a way to signify that ordinary time stopped at the minute of the death. They did not shop, do unnecessary chores, socialize at parties, go to dances, or address unnecessary affairs to observe a socially sanctioned period of mourning. Today, we can only imagine what the neighbors and extended family might think of a black wreath on the door if they even notice it.[2] In fact, because our society is so mobile, we often don't even know our neighbors to know whether they have experienced a loss let alone to recognize their particular signs of mourning.

The black wreath of mourning

[2] Unfortunately, we must be careful of placing such wreaths on the door when the house is unoccupied as the wreath may signal an opportunity for a break-in.

People of the Jewish faith have a wonderful tradition of sitting Shiva for seven days after the funeral, and this tradition truly is a gift. The bereaved stop work and remain at home for seven days of full-on mourning. They can choose to talk or not talk to those who come to sit with them. Their entitlement to these days of mourning provides an outlet for the most crucial expressions of grief. People tear an article of clothing, and they forgo unnecessary bathing, shaving, working, cooking, and the like. Covered mirrors allow them to be unconcerned with appearance. Their mourning can be quiet or it can go beyond mere tears and talk into highly expressive wailing, keening, striking out at the wind, shouting, falling prostrate to the ground, shaking one's hand and protesting "*no, no, no, no, no.*" All of these are natural and powerful responses to grief. In a cultural tradition that recognizes the importance of mourning, these primal, physical expressions are welcome.

Sadly, contemporary American society generally does not welcome or encourage such expressions of grief whether public or private. Publicly, people seem embarrassed by outwardly expressed emotions. When I wailed for my father after his casket was closed at his funeral service, a business executive's wife told me very sweetly—and kindly, to her thinking—that I needed to go "get help." What I needed, of course, was my father alive and holding me in his arms. When people faint or drop to the ground in shock, as my sister did, observers may be embarrassed and see these actions as attention seeking. In reality, though, such responses usually are honest, genuine, and very in-the-moment. They should be honored and not shamed.

In cases like these, sometimes the bereaved is encouraged to hold off expressive mourning for private times. However, when we need to wait for solitude to express grief fully, we're unable to take advantage of the sixth need of mourning, which is to allow others to help us. With a social taboo against public mourning, we may fear that we're making a spectacle, over-doing, or even dramatizing the grief *even when we are in a private place.* We may even worry that someone may find out about our need to scream in pain and think we're crazy. Let's be honest together. *Of course, mourning dramatizes grief!* Grief needs to be dramatized in ritual and instinctive expressions like wailing, keening, and public tears—and our feelings deserve such an outlet.

Wailing in grief

Grief is natural and unavoidable to humans who have loved on any level. Mourning, therefore, is a natural outlet for that grief—and it comes in many forms of expression.

The next section of this book provides a variety of practical activities that you can use for your own mourning. If what you read does not resonate as something you want to do, think about *why* that activity won't work for you. Is it because you are shy about mourning? If so, try an activity anyway to loosen up your mourning muscles. Is it because this activity is wrong for you? If so, change the activity or use what comes immediately to mind as a way to mourn for that moment or that day.

Go as slowly as you need. Mourning can be done at your own pace to meet your own unique needs. The benefits will be a fuller, richer life and a deeper capacity to love others.

Part 2

Practical Activities for Mourning

Grief is a common human experience. We are born with the capability to grieve. However, when we live in a culture that fails to acknowledge grief and where there are few good models for grief release, we can become stuck. Being stuck for a short time may be helpful when the grief is new, but staying stuck can make living well impossible. How can we learn to process and release grief?

Conscious mourning is one answer because what we first do consciously can become an unconscious, healthy, ongoing part of our lives. Here are a few examples of *healthy mourning activities*:

- Talking to people who can listen
- Crying when the need strikes
- Singing to no one and everyone
- Writing about and to the loved one
- Drawing pictures of grief, peace, or anything that fills the page
- Building sand and Lego castles; then tearing them down[3]
- Painting with large strokes and colors that fit your mood
- Creating anything
- Playing or making music for yourself or for others
- Praying and meditating

[3] This activity enacts the very impermanence of our lives. We build and tear down: nothing lasts forever.

- Screaming in a safe place like a parked car
- Throwing and breaking something of little value to release anger[4]
- Helping yourself by helping others
- Yelling at God (who has big shoulders and can handle our pain)
- Attending group meetings of similarly bereaved people

Using any one of these actions in a positive way will offer emotional, spiritual, physical, cognitive, and social releases for our grief. Releasing the grief is one way to begin to integrate a loss into our lives—to build our own healthy shell stones and strong coquina.

Negative actions are not helpful for releasing grief even though they may seem to provide temporary relief. Here are a few examples of *unhealthy mourning activities*:

- Drinking alcohol excessively
- Using recreational drugs
- Using prescription drugs inappropriately
- Shopping and spending disproportionate to one's economic means
- Gambling disproportionate to one's economic means
- Overeating or under-eating
- Purging food or other nutrients from the body
- Overworking or underworking
- Mutilating through cutting the body
- Oversleeping or under sleeping

Initially, these misguided attempts to self-medicate may seem to help because they can induce numbness or increase "high" feeling and a sense of being in the moment. However, these feelings are temporary and rely on continued self-abuse. Actions like these mask grief through destructive behaviors, thereby hurting us and those we love. Eventually, we need to confront the death and any havoc it is wreaking on our lives. Destructive mourning activities like those listed above can delay our ability to integrate the death into our lives.

---

[4] This activity works especially nicely with geodes, rocks that can be smashed to find beautiful crystals within.

In this book, I assume that the human body, mind, and spirit are connected and interconnected in various ways. Such connectedness means that the body enacts what the heart feels in grief. For example, grief can lead people to be sleepless, to oversleep, or to work excessively and into exhaustion. The mind also enacts what is happening with the emotions of grief. The result can be a kind of foggy brain or cognitive dysfunction where we begin activities but are unfocused and easily distracted. Depression can emerge as an inability to read or to think clearly. The spirit can react to grief by losing hope for the present or future. Spiritually, we can experience a faith crisis that rocks the soul or a deep sense of loss of who we are or were before our loved one's death.

Unbalanced by grief

When we understand that the body, mind, and spirit are connected, we can see that grief can unbalance us in many ways.

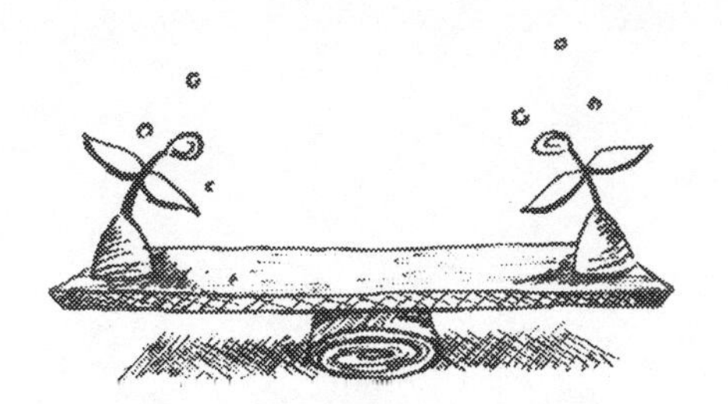

Balance restored by mourning

Mourning activities help to restore our balance.

This section of the book is organized first by five spheres or parts of our lives that particular mourning activities can touch. Chapter 3 is about activities that connect with *emotions* because emotions are what we first experience in grief. Chapter 4 provides some *spiritual* activities because we may neglect our spiritual nature for the practicalities of death. Mourning activities that address the *body* occur in chapter 5; our bodies react to grief even when our emotional and spiritual selves feel numb. Chapter 6 addresses mourning activities that engage the *mind* to give our thoughts necessary expression. Chapter 7 considers the *social* spheres of our lives. Funeral and memorial ceremonies provide us with initial social interactions, but we also need to provide social activities for ourselves a little later in our grieving processes.

This organization is not intended to suggest that everyone can or needs to address mourning in this order. In fact, these spheres can be visited whenever they feel right to you. For example, some people may find that their spirit or "soul" work needs to wait until they have done more cognitive mourning. Furthermore, there is something of a false separation among these five spheres because a mourning activity in one sphere can cross with another. For example, the body craves touch (through hugs, caresses, massage, and hand holding). Various mourning activities that engage the body also touch us emotionally (by bringing up tears or sighs), spiritually (by giving and receiving love), mentally (by clearing a cognitive space to talk about our losses), and socially (by mourning with others). Therefore, if you notice an interconnection among the five spheres, enjoy the fact that your mourning is giving you gifts that touch you on multiple levels.

Chapter 3

Mourning with Our Emotions

Using Ceremony and Ritual

Perhaps the most visible emotional mourning activity is to arrange some kind of ceremony that acknowledges our loved one's life and death. Formally committing him or her from this world to the next is a major part of accepting that a death has occurred, as we discussed in chapter 2. A ceremony is important for mourning a loved one. When we are in shock or feeling numb, a ritual that uses symbolism can speak for us. Rituals give us structure and focus when we otherwise don't know what to do or how to act.

Funeral Ceremonies and Rituals

Various professionals can help with structuring an initial funeral ceremony in a fitting way: pastors, deacons, lay bereavement ministers, and funeral directors, to name a few. Typically, these ceremonies involve some aspect of viewing and/or sitting with the deceased's body—a key way to greet the deceased in this new reality. There may be prayers, which differ in various religious settings, formal eulogies, informal words of remembrance, sacramental committal of the deceased to the next world, and some kind of internment of the body or disposition of the cremated remains. For more information about writing obituaries, eulogies, and words of remembrance, I recommend reading *Good Words: Memorializing Through a Eulogy.*

When at all possible, begin your mourning with a ceremony that allows you, as the bereaved, to encounter your loved one in death and to embrace your pain. Contemporary American society has long accepted these ceremonies as a way to let the many people who knew our loved ones say goodbye formally. Even though some of our loved ones may have asked for "celebrations" rather than funerals, our society rightly looks to funeral and memorial ceremonies as way to begin mourning. To celebrate a life before grieving its loss gets the process backwards.

How is a funeral service vital to emotion-based mourning? A funeral service acknowledges a life in a way that allows us to honor and bless our loved one. It gives us the opportunity to think and talk about this person's values, admirable characteristics, and noble deeds that we want to pass on and emulate. A funeral enables us to confront emotions, some of them unexpected. Many emotions may emerge—including pleasure and laughter as people remember the humanity of the deceased. Don't be surprised if you find yourself laughing, too. Laughter and even joking don't mean that you're being disrespectful of your beloved or other bereaved people. Grief carries with it many emotions—more than enough to fill a 64-piece crayon box.

Grief produces many emotions

Also, don't worry if the ceremony goes by in an exhausting blur. You may not consciously remember much of it, but your unconscious mind and your heart will register that you were a part of this meaningful service. When words are inadequate, humans naturally turn to ritual for comfort.

Another benefit to a funeral is that it gives us and those around us a chance to greet the deceased and say goodbye. It enables others to support us and to do something positive at a time when doing anything is a struggle. Many small and large tasks are associated with developing a ceremony. Even with the help of a skilled professional, we must make decisions that affect us emotionally. For example, we need to choose between burial or cremation of the body. In either case, we must consider when and where this action occurs.

Our hearts can tell us a lot about the need to have a public or private wake and/or viewing. If we choose a viewing, we need to decide which clothes to bring for our loved one, as well as any mementos we want to display. Will there be refreshments for mourners later? This is an important question because the breaking of bread together is a time-honored act of mutual hospitality that links us as a social group. It feeds us spiritually before we attempt to return to our daily lives where the deceased no longer works, plays, and interacts. When we eat together, we solidify our connectedness in this sorrowful time. Other decisions include how to let people know, who to call, who will write an obituary, and whether there will be a eulogy. All of these are mourning actions.

Whenever possible, I recommend a viewing because it provides a clear message to our hearts and minds that our loved one is dead—something that others in our social and family groups also will need to confront. The viewing is an important opportunity to encounter our loved one's death as a reality. It then allows us to say goodbye. When we approach a casket and talk, pray, or touch the body, we are acquainting ourselves with the deceased in her new form—a dead body that once housed her spirit of breath—which enables us to begin the process of letting go of our loved one in her human form. When people say apparently inane things like "she looks just like herself" or "I've never seen her that quiet" or "it would be better if she had her glasses on," they're not just making odd comments. They're working hard to adjust to a new reality of the deceased by voicing *how* she's different, still, cold, and unlike her living self. This opportunity can be tremendously healing.

Memorial Services

If your loved one already is gone and you didn't have the opportunity for a funeral or could not attend the service, it isn't too late to perform helpful rituals. In fact, one ceremony alone often isn't enough to fully touch the emotions—especially right after a death when we tend to be numb emotionally. You may want three or more ceremonies during the space of the first year and additional rituals that honor the deceased and your grief over the next few years—or longer.

Some of the deaths that particularly may require additional or otherwise late services include:

- Loss of a child
- Loss of a public figure
- Deaths that initially were not recognized (for example, stillborn babies, miscarriages, and abortions)
- Shocking and particularly traumatic deaths (for example, victims of murder, accidents, and terrorism)
- Socially unacceptable deaths (for example, deaths of perpetrators in the commission of a crime and illicit lovers; AIDS victims, same-sex lovers, and drug users often are included in this category although thankfully they are receiving better treatment overall)
- Military deaths that are raised to public awareness at regular times of the year

Especially elderly people or those without financial means may not have elected to have a funeral, making a memorial service particularly appropriate. Relatives of people with illness-ravaged bodies may have chosen cremation and no funeral. Victims of accidents where the physical trauma kept them from attending the original funeral for other victims often need an additional ritual or special ceremony to begin their own mourning. Situations where there are no body parts to bury or the burial occurred in another country may require multiple well-considered ceremonies because lack of a body can make it difficult to believe that the death is real and to say goodbye.

Of course, among these deaths are the ones that we ordinarily experience—our parents, children, siblings, and friends, for example. Having multiple ceremonies of different types within one year can be very helpful to engaging in emotion-based mourning.

Memorial services are popular ways to acknowledge a loved one's death using ceremony without the body being present. Sometimes these are done with the cremated remains present or with photographs and linking objects like art supplies, favorite boots, a hat, or golf clubs. Sometimes, a ceremony is held at the place of the death—such as where an accident occurred. Sometimes, it is held in the mountains or at the ocean to scatter cremated remains. A ceremony to place a headstone at a grave or a plaque at a mausoleum or to dedicate a park bench or fountain engages the bereaved, providing us with multiple opportunities to integrate our loved ones' deaths at deep, personal, emotional levels.

Mementos for a memorial ceremony

There are many opportunities to embrace ceremony with prayers, eulogies, stories of the loved one's life, and the hospitality of shared food. The difficult days of anniversaries, birthdays, and cultural holidays also provide occasions for formal candle lighting, moments of silence, or a favorite cake in the loved one's honor.

All of the activities necessary for a funeral or memorial service use our precious energy, but they begin and keep us mourning at a time when we might otherwise want to collapse into the grief. In this way, these ceremonies also give back energy. Ceremonies usefully help to keep us going as shock begins to wear off and we start to connect with our emotions.

Using Tears and Sound

> *Tears have a wisdom all their own. They come when a person has relaxed enough to let go and to work through his sorrow. They are the natural bleeding of an emotional wound, carrying the poison out of the system. Here lies the road to recovery.* F. Alexander Magoun

Crying

Mourning in ways that engage our emotions often involves tears. Some people cry freely when they grieve. In fact, sometimes they can't stop crying, and they worry about going crazy. Tears of grief typically are not signs of mental illness; indeed, they are healthy signs of mourning.

Crying can cleanse the emotions and create a sense of calm. Some researchers indicate that tears of grief or other emotional stress have different chemical components than tears produced by eye irritants like an onion or a foreign object in the eye. The chemical leucine-enkephalin may have endorphin, or natural pain relief, qualities. Although scientists are still studying tears, their chemical composition may explain why we can feel so much better—relieved and freer—after a good cry.

Crying freely is one way of self-soothing. Although it might seem that we're out of control when we cry, we actually are allowing ourselves an important form of release, which relieves grief. Along with the tears, we typically use our bodies to cry: rocking back and forth, clutching the mid-section with a self-hug, or lying down and resting after the emotional burst. If we're lucky, we'll be able to cry with someone who can hold us and provide both emotional and physical support.

The emotional support of a hug

Some people don't cry in grief. That isn't a sign of sickness or being abnormal. Some people simply aren't criers in general. People who haven't cried during most of their lives may not cry when bereaved—and they shouldn't be judged as mourning inadequately. If you're deeply bereaved and not crying worries you, ask yourself whether you were a person who cried easily before this loss (or other losses). If not, then you most likely are responding in your own unique way. Additionally, as we discussed in chapter 1, it's important to remember that sometimes relief is the most natural emotional response at the death of a loved one—often with good reason. Tears may or may not come with a sense of relief.

Typically, tears—if they're going to come—will flow in their own good time and often when they're least expected. There's no hurry or rush about this emotional response to grief. As one book title says so wonderfully, there is no wrong way to cry.[5]

Using Sound to Feel and Release Emotions

There are times when a bereaved person wants to cry and cannot. In fact, sometimes people are both unable to cry *and* to talk about their losses. Such speechlessness seems to come from pent-up pain and fear of releasing that pain. Sometimes people think that their feelings are so awful or powerful that they shouldn't be voiced. There are times when a person might want to talk about the grief but is afraid to use her voice lest the tears come. In this case, the person can feel stuck and frustrated.

---

[5] Joe Kempf, *No One Cries the Wrong Way (*Huntington, IN: Our Sunday Visitor, 2002).

There are ways to mourn vocally that can release emotion and clear out some of the difficult feelings associated with grief. Sometimes tears come with the sounds.

Wailing, keening, and screaming in grief are age-old mourning actions. Wailing often is described as an animal-like sound that releases pain, grief, or anger. Keening is a vocal lament that may sound like a death song or poem. In some traditions, a leader would keen and others would follow up with a chorus. Keening customarily is done over the deceased's body at a wake or at a grave. Screaming is a common sound made when we are frightened, shocked, or protesting a reality. Screams can release a great deal of emotion—often mixed feelings that otherwise feel unmanageable. Most of us likely have seen movies or television shows—if not real life—where bereaved people make these powerful sounds.

Making uncontrolled noise, which may be disconcerting to those who hear it, is a healthy way to engage grief positively. Our society, as we discussed in chapter 2, tends to be uncomfortable with expressive displays of emotion. However, emotional and noisy expressions are natural, normal, and often necessary for humans in grief.

How can we make these mourning sounds? Give yourself permission to let loose and be loud if you feel like screaming or sobbing. Sometimes, just letting the sound out a few times will bring on a sense of crying out pain.

Wailing, keening, and screaming release pain, which leaves our hearts more open. If you stop here, you may feel like you have a terrible hole in the heart. Instead, if possible, ask someone you trust to hold you. Hold that person after the sound stops and then breathe quietly for as long as possible. If a person isn't available, try holding a willing pet after the sounds are out. Holding and being held can fill that open space with love and peace. As bereaved people, we need to fill ourselves up with good feelings whenever possible, so this is a wonderful time for getting support from another.

When a grief burst has interrupted your sense of balance, try to find a safe place for a few quick screams that let out emotion. For example, you can go to your car, turn on the radio (with the ignition off) to mask sound, and use your voice to scream or wail or cry. Give yourself time to recover afterwards, and the day may feel more possible.

> Try not to censor your emotions. We have enough different emotions to fill a large crayon box! All of these emotions have a place in our lives. Feel them. Use them. Heal them.

Using Symbols to Express Emotions

Speaking out emotions—another way to make sounds—can provide significant relief. For example, one reason that some people like grief support groups is that they can use words to share their emotions and grief experiences.

When words are not enough or when they are not possible, symbols speak for us. Common cultural symbols provide a mutually understandable language. A white pall on a casket symbolizes the purity of baptism for Christians. A Star of David on a headstone symbolizes that a Jewish person is buried there. Angels or figures with wings symbolize the belief in or hope for an afterlife. Wheels symbolize the cycle of death and rebirth for Buddhists. The hour glass symbolizes the passage of time as do lit candles. A Masons', Daughters of the American Revolution, or Odd Fellows' symbol at a funeral signifies the death of a member of one of those societies. An American flag on a casket symbolizes an honor to a former or current member of the Unites States' Armed Forces.

People associate many symbols with their loved ones. Such associations can take emotions that otherwise hold us hostage and give them voice. When our voices are least trustworthy, ceremonies, ritual, and symbols speak for us.

The following are some symbolic ways to express emotions.

Build a Memorial

Humans memorialize death in many concrete ways. We have all seen cemetery headstones, statues, and war memorials. These monuments create a sacred space out of the ordinary place or object. In such places, people behave differently, quietly, reverently. Headstones can lift up our loved one and allow us to look outward rather than downward to the grave. One example of a deeply touching memorial is the twin, black, V-shaped walls dedicated to Vietnam War veterans in Washington, D.C. Another example is the U.S. Holocaust Museum, also in Washington, D.C., that honors the more than twelve million people murdered during the Nazi holocaust.

The grave as a memorial

At such memorials, people mourn the dead, talk to them, and reflect on their place in our lives—both personally and socially. In fact, such memorials give people an opportunity to mourn their own suffering. They teach us about the past and provide public ways to remember someone. Memorializing is a ritualistic statement of our solidarity as a society in that we share certain shared beliefs about the sacredness of life and the honor due to the dead.

With larger monuments to people and events, we typically take months or years after the event to reflect and plan before designing and building a memorial. For cemetery memorials, gravestones typically are placed within a few weeks to months of the death. For those in the Jewish faith, up to a year may pass before a headstone placing ceremony occurs, which also marks a formal end to the socially supported mourning period. This practice can help with the emotions of grief because it combines both the value of ceremony and a year's maturity as mourners of this particular death mark a milestone year of mourning.

In a society that disregards death, there can be a rush to memorialize. It's possible to place a memorial too early. An example is that of a roadside memorial to signal that a loved one died at that spot. The placing of a cross, other symbols, or flowers on that spot may seem critical at that time, and it often garners the kind of attention a loved one's death requires: visits, flowers, memorabilia left by the road. In the long run, however, the memorial itself doesn't satisfy the needs of mourning fully. First, it isn't permanent and a road crew might remove it at any time. In fact, these memorials are forbidden by law in some states as a distraction to drivers. Second, and more importantly, roadside memorials mark the place of death—always a reminder of tragedy—rather than a place of rest. They don't represent a movement toward integrating the loss into our lives. Planning and creating something more permanent can help with mourning emotionally.

A memorial along the roadside

While roadside memorials are quite popular responses to deadly accidents, they're immediate responses to a loss and not a permanent memorial to the deceased loved one. If we develop memorials too early, they can be used as crutches to avoid pain. Then, when pain returns, there can be an urge to develop yet another memorial to quash that pain. A cycle of pain avoidance is harmful to integrating the death fully.

Remember that we can't avoid pain in grief. It is best, then, to embrace the pain—make a friend of it—and feel it deeply in order to live more fully in the future. The pain will not always be as intense as it is when you begin to mourn actively. The process of mourning will soften the pain. Take your time in designing and creating a memorial. Then, if you feel the need, memorialize more than once. Trust your emotions to tell you what you need to know about memorials.

Some of the memorials that my family and I have generated include:

- Planting an American Elm dedicated to my brother and father
- Planting two Paper Birch trees in honor of my mother-in-law and father-in-law
- Placing a memorial placard on a favorite garden bench in honor of my sister
- Putting angel figures all around these trees and in the garden

Other people we know have:

- Planted special flowers or a garden in honor of their loved ones
- Built a fountain in the town square for their parents, who were central to the town's development and survival
- Dedicated a children's play park to a deceased child
- Dedicated a dog park to a beloved pet

A fountain memorial

Memorials allow our emotions to have concrete expression in a public way and they say to everyone that *she lived*, *he was loved*, and *their lives mattered*. They teach us and inspire others.

Three Stones

It's important to mourn our loved ones authentically and with integrity. Sometimes, this means recalling and talking about edgy or difficult times in the relationship. The "Three Stones" exercise uses stones as symbols to help with this goal of honest mourning.

Find three stones. You can buy them at a store for gemstones or pick them up from a local park. Holding the three stones, decide which one you think is most beautiful. Which one seems ordinary? Which of the three is the least attractive or even ugly? This is an exercise where beauty truly is in the eye of the beholder. The idea is to find the richness of a full life with your beloved deceased and not just the good or bad stories that we tell ourselves over and over.

Symbolizing a life with three stones

- Use the beautiful stone to voice a good memory of your loved one. Talk about why this memory is so special. This stone represents the wonderful and special memories that you want to keep.
- Use the ordinary stone to connect with a neutral or commonplace memory like how she made dinner or how he dressed for school. Describe your feelings connected with the ordinary memory.
- Then, use the least attractive stone to find an unpleasant memory of your loved one. It could deal with a bad habit or a hospital trauma. This kind of connection is something we may want to forget about, but because it also formed the life you shared with your loved one, it's important for having a complete and realistic memory of your time together.

Talk with someone about the images and feelings that you have related to these stones. Or, write about them in a journal. Share them with a grief support group. In some way, use words to externalize the feelings these images raise. Taken together, these stones can symbolize pieces (never the whole) of a life spent loving someone special. Sometimes emotions like guilt or anger may come up, but also we may feel sadness, happiness, and peace through this exercise. These feelings may signal that there's a particular emotion we need to address or an event that we need to confront. Part of mourning is accepting that no relationship is perfect and that we may need to remember and work through parts of the past.

> If feelings like guilt arise, remember that guilty feelings sometimes mask a sense of helplessness about not being able to "save" a loved one from pain or death.

Photographs

Photos are powerful symbols of our love and grief. We take photos with our cameras, with our phones, and with our computers. We also take mental snapshots when no camera is around. Our minds produce memories from those mental pictures. However, these are hard to share with others, which is why visual images are superior. Here are some ways to use photographs as emotional symbols of grief.

Slowly go through old photos to find the ones that most show your loved one at her best. Place them in one pile. Then, look for those photos that are silly—where the camera captured your loved one with a look on her face that she would have hated to see. Place them in another pile. Look for other photos that reveal different emotions in your loved one: anger, sadness, joy, pain, loving, kindness, and the like. Place these in other piles. What you're doing is confronting your emotions by viewing your loved one in all her emotional states. Allow yourself to feel whatever arises because these feelings are part of your mourning. You can stop at this point, or:

- Use these photos to create a collage of your loved one as a whole human being—not just at her "best." Although we all like to see ourselves in "good" photos, as bereaved people, we have to remember that our loved ones were multidimensional and complete people. While it's common to make our loved ones into saints, they weren't perfect. For mourning purposes, it helps to remember that.

- Make a box of different snapshots for various family members and, providing them with an album, let them build their own memories by putting their albums together.
- Create a traditional paper-based scrapbook of photographic memories.
- Scan snapshots created with negatives and use other digital images to make an original hardcover photo book for loved ones. These are easy to make and relatively inexpensive at local drug stores—check their online Websites. Make one and replicate it for as many people as you like or individualize the photo books for different bereaved family members. Make a book for each child, for example; it becomes special by choosing photos particular to that child with the loved one. To make the task simpler, place the same photos of the loved one at end of the book.
- Share your favorite photos on a Facebook album or through another social networking page. Include a few words about why these show your loved one in a way that is memorable to you. Invite comments, but encourage people to be sensitive in the what they write. The comments should be appropriate for all readers. Likewise, if you're invited to comment on someone else's photos and stories, please write comments that will not shock or hurt principle mourners like parents, grandparents, and spouses.
- Take old videos and have them remediated to create a YouTube video on the Internet. Check the Internet for companies that take film movies and video tapes, converting them to DVD and/or movie files. After putting the files on YouTube or another video-ready site, share the URL with people that you believe will understand your emotions. You can even share the video with people that you're having difficulty talking to; sometimes this less personal venue allows people to do some

of their own mourning and grieving in a way that doesn't interfere with yours.

- If the funeral or memorial service was video recorded, share it online with family and friends who couldn't attend. Doing so shares the opportunity to say goodbye through a ceremony and opens the door to connect emotionally about the deceased and your own grief.
- Place photos of your loved one around the house. Look for a balance between showing as many photos as you want and plastering the walls completely with this person's photo. Try not to "stop time" with only this loved one showcased in your home as it isn't healthy to remember him or her to the exclusion of the living people you love and who love you.
- Frame a special photo for other family members who otherwise may not have access to it. Choose different ones that would have particular meaning for each person.
- Frame a photograph with a poem or the eulogy or other words that aptly describe what you're feeling about your loved one.

> *There is a sacredness in tears. They are not the mark of weakness, but of power. They speak more eloquently than ten thousand tongues. They are the messengers of overwhelming grief... and unspeakable love.* Washington Irving

Angel Talk

Although angels are a known spiritual symbol, for many people, the idea of angels isn't about the spirit as much as about their emotional needs for connecting with the loved one in the next world. In this case, there's a clear intersection of the mourning spheres.

Angel connections

- Talking to an angel—for example, one's guardian angel—can be one way to work consciously with grief emotions. Close your eyes and imagine that your loved one is in the heavenly presence of an angel. Thank the angel for watching over your beloved. Then, with the angel acting as an intermediary between you and your loved one, tell your loved one what you are experiencing. Begin with a line like, "*Let me tell you what life has been like since you died.*" Share your full crayon box of emotions. Then, stop and listen. In your emotional self, is your loved one talking back to you? What is he or she telling you?
- Collect angel figures, broaches, pendants, or artwork. Use angel stationary for sending hand-written letters. You can select the artistic form that best suits your sense of angel as symbol. There might be different angels for different emotions that you experience in grief. Is the angel a guardian? Fierce? Strong? Vengeful? Joyful? Peaceful? Allow the imagery to help you experience your emotions. Remember that the angel isn't an idol but a symbol of the emotions you are addressing in this mourning activity.

When you see a penny on the ground, pick it up and place it in a special container. My special container is a hand-thrown, lidded pot that a friend made after my brother died. It's about one third full of coins at this point. When I find a penny, I ask myself which loved one might be thinking of me or could be especially proud of me that day. When I find more than one coin, I think about whether my actions might have pleased more than one of my loved ones. When I find a dime or a quarter, I use that discovery to wonder what I might have done especially well that a loved one might tell me about. These "angel pennies" are one way to connect with our loved ones through our positive emotions—a coinage pat on the back.

Collecting angel pennies

Forgiveness

We cannot underestimate the power of forgiveness, and practicing forgiveness is a powerful emotional mourning activity. Every one of us has someone to forgive for a transgression: something said or left unsaid, a bad deed, or a disappointment that has become bitterness. The loss of a loved one through death brings home the brevity of our lives.

> *Only people who are capable of loving strongly can also suffer great sorrow, but this same necessity of loving serves to counteract their grief and heals them.* Leo Tolstoy

- As emotions sift and settle in grief, perhaps the most important emotional mourning activity is to forgive. Sometimes our loved ones have done bad things that are difficult to forgive, especially if they haven't been addressed overtly. If you can, forgive the deceased or forgive a family member who has disappointed you during the dying or grieving period. Forgive yourself if you wish you had done something differently because regret can keep us entrenched in the past. Forgiveness is a high act of love and reverence for the deceased and for us.

- Try this forgiveness meditation:

  Close your eyes and breathe deeply. Imagine that you are on a plane flying over the ocean. The ocean is vast and it nurtures many animals and beautiful vegetation. It has more than enough space to hold your grief. In fact, ocean animals will gobble it up so that it doesn't pollute their world. Pack up your anger, disappointment, sadness, or other emotions too heavy, too sad, or too fragile to bear on your grief journey. Pack them into a cardboard box. Strap yourself safely into the plane and open an exit door. Toss the box out of the plane as the wind ruffles your clothes and messes your hair. Wave goodbye to these jettisoned emotions. When you leave the plane, remember that these particular emotions are gone. In their place is deep forgiveness.

- Forgive as many people as you want and as often as you like. Forgiveness opens our hearts to positive emotions like no other mourning activity. It has the added benefit of cleaning our hearts and minds of old and unneeded negative memories.

Other Emotion-Based Mourning Activities

- When you feel a need to cry or think about your loved one, set a timer for fifteen minutes and let yourself go. Then, when the timer rings, collect yourself and your thoughts to continue the day. Do this as often as needed. The timer helps us to balance mourning with daily life.
- Reach out to others in need. It's a sure-fire way to bring your own emotions to the surface, which allows you to recognize and work with them. You'll be doing something good for someone else at the same time.
- Cuddle or pet an animal. There's something very comforting about holding a compliant animal and talking out emotions.

- Sleep with a piece of your loved one's clothing. The scent, texture, and size of a shirt, scarf, or other item can be enormously comforting because our senses signal emotional memories that need to be acknowledged.
- Do something pleasurable daily to improve your mood. We must remind our emotions of good feelings even if for a short time.
- Listen to music. Music shared with your now deceased loved one might evoke sad feelings and tears. Other music may calm rough emotions. Music appeals to the senses that also respond to the emotions.
- Go on retreat. Retreat houses like *Chapel House* at the Colgate University in New York and the *Washington Retreat House* in Washington, D.C. are hospitable places where the bereaved are welcome. Activities can help emotionally and spiritually as grief is explored in these safe spaces.
- Find a therapist or grief coach, if needed. A trained professional can greatly assist you with grief-bound emotions.
- If your emotions remain stuck, try the absurd. Buy water-based finger-paints, put on a swimsuit, and get into the bathtub. Tape a large sheet of paper on the wall. The bathtub wall can be a wondrously large canvas for painting out fear, anger, pain, and confusion. This is an especially good activity to engage a child's emotions and open up communication. If the bathroom wall won't work, large sheets of paper on a safe floor remain the mainstay of finger-painting. Wash up the tub and any spilled paint quickly, however, or you may find another reason to be angry!

What other mourning activities can address your emotions?

Chapter 4

Mourning with Our Spirits

According to Pierre Teilhard de Chardin in *The Phenomenon of Man,* "We are not human beings on a spiritual journey. We are spiritual beings on a human journey." In other words, our spiritual selves are engaged in human experience, which can be both delightful and very hard. Part of the natural, normal, and necessary human experience is to grieve our dead. Ultimately, each of us also will die. The death of our loved ones reminds us of our own mortality, an uncomfortable truth.

The word "spirit" has many different meanings. Our spirits provide us with hope, courage, vigor, and the capacities to love, empathize, and sympathize with others. Spirit is what enables us to form meaningful relationships with others, with ourselves, and with God. For some, the idea of having a spirit equates with having a soul, and it distinguishes humans from other animals. For others, the spirit is the literal breath of life that leaves our eyes when we die and stop breathing. Spirit is, as Dr. Wolfelt suggests, the divine spark within each of us. Spirit lives both in our human bodies now and beyond them in the next world. In this chapter, we'll look at various ways of mourning that connect us spiritually with the deceased, with ourselves, with others, and with God (or your conception of a Higher Being). Here I simply call this Higher Being *God.*

> *How can he be said to have died, he who lives in my heart?* St. Augustine

It's important to know that our spirits may be very low and in a "dark night of the soul," a spiritual crisis, while we grieve. We ask "why did this happen?" and wonder how a good God could let our loved ones die, let them die how they did, or allow us to live without them. Yet, while we struggle with that darkness, we also yearn to connect with our loved ones spiritually, which is one way of seeking the light. And, although relighting that divine spark within us may take quite some time, we still can practice spirit-based activities that enact mourning and invite connection with our beloved deceased.

Connecting with the Deceased

How do people maintain a connection with the deceased? To connect means to join or link up. In this sense, our spirits are joined forever to others, specifically to the deceased. This kind of connection requires only our conscious intention to maintain a relationship with our loved ones beyond this world. To paraphrase St. Augustine, those who continue to live in my heart are not dead except in their bodily form. This heart-based connection is, I think, a type of interdependence among humans—alive and dead—and it is how we stay connected beyond death.

Tradition and Spiritual Connection

Just as when we mourn with our emotions, tradition provides us with many ways to connect spiritually with our loved ones, especially in the early days of loss. These include such mourning activities as participating in the ceremonial ritual of a wake, funeral, memorial service, sitting Shiva, and the unveiling of a headstone or other memorial.

Western tradition used to dictate that we bury our deceased in the hallowed ground of a churchyard or other consecrated cemetery. Contemporary American society has more recently adapted some Eastern practices of cremation with a preference for interring the cremated remains of the body (often called *cremains*) in a special columbarium or in the ground. New technology and practices have led to people storing some of the deceased's remains in ash-containing jewelry, manufactured gemstones that bond the carbon from ashes, and stylish urns intended for permanent display. Although these ways of individualizing the death and connecting with the deceased are contested among various religious groups and within families, they're becoming quite popular among the bereaved.

Interring our loved ones

These practices can support mourning in healthy ways if there's an intention to heal behind them. However, it seems important to do something meaningful with the deceased's remains. Some faiths require that a body or cremated remains be interred in a consecrated place like a cemetery, mausoleum niche, or columbarium. Some people don't believe this kind of interment is necessary. Rather than inter their cremated loved ones, they keep the deceased in their homes. Some plan to scatter the ashes at a future date and others wait to make a decision or leave the decision to later generations.

In unusual choices, I've heard of people taking their loved ones on a "road trip" across the country or keeping them in places like the computer cupboard. Some bereaved people (particularly parents of somewhat wayward deceased children) have expressed to me that they want to know exactly where the deceased is and that they find comfort by looking in the cupboard and finding the loved one's remains there. Others worry that if they inter their loved one and later have to move to another state or country, they will lose all physical connection with their loved ones. Truly, our desire to know where our loved ones now reside is powerful, and if we don't know where the spirit lives, many of us will settle for knowing where the ashes are kept.

Religious concerns aside, the decision of whether to inter cremains, to keep them, or to scatter them is very personal. However, I think it's important to let go of the deceased loved one's remains at some point. Eventually, the symbolic nature of interring the ashes should be considered. Other family members may want or need to have some place to visit the deceased and pay respects. The value of a family cemetery plot, for example, is that later generations can visit and connect with their family members.

Here are some possible ways to honor the deceased when the remains are cremated:

- Ceremonially inter the remains in a grave, mausoleum, or columbarium after the funeral service.
- Keep the remains in an urn in a place of honor in your home as long as that is comforting. Surround the remains with photographs or linking objects, making that place sacred to the loved one's memory. Invite family members to have private and quiet time with the loved one's cremated remains.
- Decide whether to scatter, inter, or keep the remains during your life time. If you keep them, provide written instructions for what family members are to do after your death. For example, do you want the remains interred in a grave or columbarium? Do you want them interred with you? Do you want them scattered with your own remains? Consider the needs of other family members so that they don't have to ask, "*Now what am I supposed to do with Gramps and Aunt Nel?*"
- If you choose to scatter the cremated remains, decide how you will include elements of ceremony and whether other family members will be invited. If possible, leave some kind of a marker at the place of release so that you and others can visit this now sacred place.

Talking with Our Loved Ones

People who aren't mourning might not understand a desire to talk to a deceased loved one, but talking is one of the most powerful ways that we connect with them spiritually. For example, you might lie on the grave with an ear to the ground or look at the urn and tell the deceased what you're experiencing. While the deceased won't respond in audible words, you may find some answers in the silence. In fact, sometimes answers are already in your heart and in your unconscious self, and you can imagine that the beloved whispers in your ears.

When people ask in grief group how they can know that their loved ones hear them, I say:

> *Imagine that your deceased loved one is sitting on your shoulder. Tell him or her what you're worried about. I know that you may not know what decision to make about fixing the plumbing or buying a new car or selling the house or how to take best care of your child. These are difficult decisions, and it can be hard to know what to do. But, you may find that you have a good sense of what he or she would say if you sit with the silence for a while. Listen to your heart. Listen with your heart.*

Although this communication of the heart may not always bear fruit, sometimes we can talk and listen to our loved ones as a productive way to mourn.

Some bereaved people may not have known the deceased well enough to have a heart-felt sense of what he or she would say about a concern or need. Losing a parent early in life is one of those situations, while losing a new friend is another. In these cases, it may be helpful to talk with someone who knew that person better. Talking about what the beloved might have said or thought can be difficult, but it also can open new relationships and lead to a satisfying sense that the deceased still matters.

Connecting with Ourselves

Breathing

When we grieve, the divine spark of our spirits dim, just as an overturned cup dims a candle flame, causing it to struggle for oxygen. Grief literally can make us completely breathless, as it did for my sister upon viewing my brother's body in the casket. Both literally and figuratively, we bereaved may find ourselves walking the world as shadows, silently protesting the death, and behaving as if we're the ghosts. To help us, the very first task of mourning spiritually through self-connection is to breathe. In this sense, breathing is more than a physical requirement for living. It's critical to *being*.

Watch a baby breathe. The little belly rises and falls—filling like a balloon—with each breath. As babies, we begin life with deep belly breaths. As we go through life, we tend to breathe higher and higher into our bodies until, just before death, we breathe in our throats, barely reaching the lungs. Baby-belly breathing is necessary when mourning because the life-giving oxygen goes straight to the diaphragm and fills all our blood cells.

Remarkably, breathing is surprisingly easy to forget. If you doubt that, stop reading right now and focus on your breath. How deeply are you breathing in? Are you breathing out deeply? Is this constant breathing, or are you holding your breath when you read difficult passages in this book? Take a few minutes right now and breathe deeply.

On a regular basis—which will help to set a new habit—try breathing deeply with something in your hands. I use *Bead Blessings*, a mourning-focused set of healing beads.[6] Each set of beads has a dragonfly, butterfly, tree of life, sankofa,[7] or some other hope-based symbol. While I hold the beads, I breathe in deeply and breathe out deeply and slowly, centering my thoughts. My primary goal is to reconnect with myself in this breathing exercise. Sometimes I focus on the connection I have to

---

[6] *Bead Blessings* are handmade for bereavement work by Dawn Hammerbacher and Charlotte Robidoux. See http://www.goodwordsforgrieving.com/bead-blessings/

[7] A sankofa is a symbol from Ghana that means "look-back bird," and it conveys that we should "go back and get it." In chapter 6, I discuss this symbol and how it provides a healthy message about incorporating the past into our current lives.

the person I am mourning. Other times, I concentrate on the beauty of the natural world around me and give thanks for its abundance.

***Bead Blessing*: An elephant never forgets and you don't have to either**

***Bead Blessing*: I will miss you always**

Another object to hold while breathing is a linking object, which is a tangible item like an article of clothing, a stuffed animal, or another thing that belonged to a loved one. My favorite linking item is a slide rule that belonged to my father, who was an electrical engineer. It slips into a battered, forest-green, leather case that I like to touch to my cheek when I miss him particularly. It's cool, smooth, and intimately reminds me of Dad's life and gentle touch with me.

It also can be helpful spiritually to recite a mantra while breathing. A mantra is an utterance made sacred by our intentions. One mantra that I like to use is designed to help us remember to breathe. Focus on your breath as you gently breathe in and out. Before reciting this mantra, try making the sound *AH* as you expel a breath. Now it may be easier *to feel the breathing.*

1. Breathe in: *How do I live without my beloved?*
2. Breathe out: *One breath at a time.*
3. Breathe in: *How do I go on?*
4. Breathe out: *One minute at a time.*
5. Breathe in: *How does the Earth keep turning?*
6. Breathe out: *One hour at a time.*
7. Breathe in: *How will I find peace?*
8. Breathe out: *One day at a time.*

Self-Connection with Symbols

When a loved one dies, we lose a part of identities. It's important not only to remain connected to our loved ones, but also to ourselves. One way to do that is through symbolic identification as a bereaved person. Some of the mourning traditions that identify us as bereaved are rarer than they once were:

- Wearing black clothes (or the color clothing that indicates mourning in your culture)
- Wearing a black armband
- Pinning a mourning broach (such as an angel, dragonfly, butterfly, or photo of the loved one) to clothes or a purse
- Covering the mirrors in the house to signify that appearance is not as important as the mourning
- Lighting candles in honor of the deceased
- Lighting a candle to speak about the deceased—one candle per family member

Since these are rarer activities, their meaning is especially strong. For example, what we wear says something about us and people notice what we wear. Therefore, wearing black or other specific colored clothes for a period after a death indicates a purposeful connection to our loved ones. The same could be said for wearing an article of the loved one's clothes. In other words, because society does not require or expect these mourning actions any longer, the connection actually becomes more powerful.

Wearing a memorial necklace or bracelet that includes a charm that our loved ones cherished or a photograph of a loved one is another symbolic way to connect with ourselves as a bereaved person. Such items also can be attached to a bridal bouquet on the wedding day. There are many jewelry makers who can construct such mementos. For example, photographer and designer Robin Sommers made the bracelet and bridal pendant shown here.[8]

Bridal bouquet with memorial photo

[8] For information about Robin Sommer's work, see Cool Chick Photo Jewelry at www.robinsommer.com.

Memorial photo bracelet

Finding Gratitude

Another way to become and remain connected to our spiritual selves is through gratitude. I know that confronting a loved one's death usually doesn't lead to gratitude, but finding appreciation can be critical for a healthy spirit and to mourn spiritually. The following ideas may help you to remember your connection to those events that cause you gratitude.

- Think of the pleasure and joy that emanates from a child's hug. If you can find a child with whom you have a relationship, ask for a hug and respond in kind.
- Look at spring flowers that grow with the blessing of sunshine and water droplets. These prove that life continues. If it isn't spring, go to a florist shop, a greenhouse, or an arboretum. Life continues in all seasons.
- Notice the kindness of people. Some will be kind to you because you are bereaved. Others will be kind out of their very nature. In the most unexpected places, you will find kindness. Wash yourself in the niceness that you find.
- Shower your own appreciations and blessings on others. Everyone needs a blessing sometime. Sit on the bus or subway to work, look at as many people as possible, and silently bless that person's day, wishing for them the very best. Uplift your own spirit through your generosity.
- Eat small amounts of high-quality dark chocolate. It tastes wonderful, and it contains phenyl ethylamine, a chemical that releases endorphins in the brain, making you feel better temporarily. By the way, although it may take a little time to

acquire taste for it, dark chocolate with its high cocoa count is healthier than milk chocolate.

- Go to a grocery store and consider all of the good food that it contains. For just a few dollars, most of us can afford healthy, appetizing food. Because we are still alive, individual health challenges notwithstanding, we have the ability to eat nutritious food.

Connecting with Others

Social Needs for Spiritual Connection

Grief can cause a spiritual rupture within us, and it can affect our relationships with others. Particularly in families, it's important to connect on spiritual levels that often preclude words but sometimes require them. As chapter 7 discusses, grief isn't only an individual experience, but also a social one. Just as we need to connect spiritually with our loved ones and ourselves, we need to connect socially. Interacting with other humans helps us to mourn more fully. One way to achieve this connection is to go on a retreat with family or other bereaved people. Retreats are time away from the daily chores of life, usually in a place other than home. They can bring about a strong sense of the sacred. Retreats don't have to happen at a religious house like a monastery to be sacred or spiritually healing. Fruitful and delightful retreats can occur at the beach, in the woods, or in other potentially quiet places that lend themselves to stopping time temporarily for reflection and rejuvenation.

Another way to connect spiritually with others is to work in groups with various mourning activities. When two or more people work to create something together, their work opens a space for talking about the deceased. People who normally won't talk about the spiritual nature of their grief may do so in a social setting. Talking about our tears—how we cry and why—is both an emotional and a spiritual connector with others.

Tear Jars

Another type of group activity that addresses the spirit is to decorate tear bottles or jars. Tear jars were made in ancient Greece as well as in the Middle East of the Old Testament. In their hot, dry climates, water was especially important to life. Tears were considered a sacrificial gift from one's own body. People caught these tears in tiny bottles and jars, and the tears were used like holy water to bless and cool. When the tear jar owner had experienced a significant death—a parent, sibling, child, or spouse—it could be decorated. The grief was a rite of passage after which it was understood that the person would never be the same. Their decorated tear bottle was an indication that they had the necessary experience to be with others who grieved deeply. Interestingly, there also is a Judeo-Christian tradition of catching precious tears, which God values as evidence of our troubles. In Psalm 56, verse 8, the psalmist says:

> *My wanderings you have noted;*
> *Are my tears not stored in your vial,*
> *Recorded in your book?* [New American *Bible*]

Tear jar of grief

Making tear jars is easy. Use small bottles the size of perfume atomizers, tiny body oil bottles, or miniature bottles found in hotel rooms and on airplanes. With permanent markers, color the bottles in the colors and styles most representative of the person you lost. Then, if you want, brush on liquid sparkles found in the fabric painting aisle of a fabric or craft store. You can make and individualize more than one tear jar to signify multiple losses. For example, after Virginia Tech's tragic murders in 2007, I made a tear bottle in the school's colors with a *VT* on it for my son, a bereaved and deeply shocked graduate of the university.

Admire the tear jars of others because these decorations come from deep inside us and reflect our spiritual connections to our loved ones. Keep your tear jar in a special place like a shrine for your loved one.

Hand-decorated tear jars

Connecting with the Highest Being

Asking "Why?"

As we know, it's important to face the grief even at the risk of pain. Our losses can reveal a gaping hole in our spirits, filled only by God. That hole may have existed before losing the loved one to death and the grief makes it more obvious and tangible. Additionally, grief can generate terrible spiritual pain, often characterized by the question *Why?* We ask this question not of our loved ones, ourselves, or our social group. We ask *why* of God. Although we may not ever find out *why*, we must ask.

> *To spare oneself from grief at all cost can be achieved only at the price of total detachment, which excludes the ability to experience happiness.* Erich Fromm

A Crusade to Right Wrongs

Finding meaning in a death can be difficult. We want to know why our loved one died, and we want an answer *now*. Our emotions cry out for a sense of justice—particularly when the death was unnecessary as with an automobile accident or a murder. Our minds also seek logic in illogical tricks of fate, such as why our loved one died from a disease such as the measles, flu, or pneumonia when millions of other people heal. Most of all, our spirits seek a sense of peace in doing something—anything—about the death. These are reasons why people crusade against what they perceive as wrong. They want to make good come from evil and life come from death.

For example:

- In 1980, Candace Lightner founded Mothers Against Drunk Driving (MADD) after her thirteen-year old daughter was killed by a drunk driver who had been arrested previously for drinking and driving. This non-profit organization not only educates people about drunk driving, it also lobbies for legislation that stiffens the consequences for drunk drivers.
- In 1994, Megan Kanka, a seven-year old girl was raped and murdered by a repeat offender. A national bill was sponsored by those who were shocked by her death; it passed and now sex offenders have to register as sex offenders where they live.
- The Adam Walsh Child Protection and Safety Act was signed into federal law in 2006. This act, spurred on by the tragic death of eight-year old Adam Walsh who was kidnapped from a Florida mall in 1981, places sex offenders into three categories and mandates their registration according to these categories. Walsh's father, John Walsh, has spent most of his life since his son was murdered fighting this kind of crime. He founded the National Center for Missing and Exploited Children (NCMEC) and hosted *America's Most Wanted.*
- Janet Manion founded the Travis Manion Foundation in 2007 in honor of her son, a lieutenant in the Marine Corps who died saving fellow service members in Iraq. This foundation provides fellowships and scholarships for wounded and disabled veterans.

These are only a few of many good people who have taken the tragic loss of their loved ones and attempted to make something positive from the pain. Not all of the scholarships, foundations, and organizations have achieved national recognition, but they are developed in honor of someone who died and they typically help the living in the name of that person. For example, hospitals have newly built wings and schools have equipment that come from local organizations involved in memorializing the deceased. The bereaved know that they have done something good in remembrance of their loved ones. Crusading feeds the bereaved spirit, emotions, and brain; it gives the bereaved something physical to do and attempts to aid society overall.

There's a danger for the bereaved, however, in a crusade that occurs too quickly or becomes all encompassing. Like the roadside memorial to the dead, the crusade can receive a lot of attention and require the full focus of the bereaved. Nonetheless, it's important not to avoid the grief or allow this work to displace the essential work of mourning on the personal level that grief requires. The bereaved crusader can become so wrapped up in the hard work of changing the circumstances that enabled the loved one's death that they can forget to take time to mourn and heal. Later, when they least expect to have to address it, grief will come seeking the attention it hasn't yet received.

There are many facets to mourning—especially in the spiritual realm—and it's vital to pay attention to all of these facets. If you decide to crusade to right a wrong or to honor your loved one, please also take time for the hard work of simply mourning this death. Grief needs much attention, and it'll wait for attention to be paid. Years down the road, that grief will be waiting until it has been fully mourned.

Prayer and Meditation

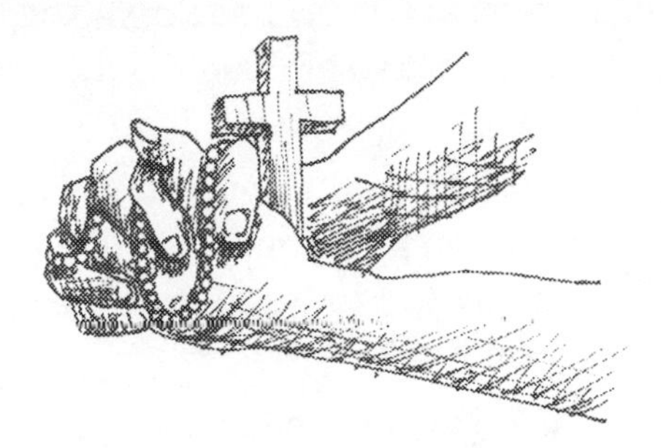

Talking to God with prayer

Questions of *why* suggest that no matter how much we may try, we cannot completely detach from the human need for God. Our spiritual lives cry for this. Prayer is one response that can reconnect or connect us more deeply to God when we're in pain. Meditation is another. In my spiritual tradition, prayer is talking with God. Meditation, which is part of deep prayer, is sitting with the prayer and listening to what God answers. In most meditation, one strives to connect with a Higher Being. The following are some ways to pray and meditate to connect spiritually with God:

- Talk to a spiritual mentor: a priest, minister, deacon, sister—anyone who has developed a firm connection with God in your spiritual tradition. Be honest about your fears, anger, and sadness. These people have wisdom to share that can be helpful when we allow it to happen.
- Have a special church service offered in memory of the loved one. In a Catholic Mass, for example, the deceased's name will be said at the altar in memorial and everyone in the church will be praying for this person—and by extension, for the family and loved ones.
- Pray frequently using whatever words suit your needs. Remember that we can pray in petition, in appreciation, in thanksgiving, and in praise.
- Hold onto positive and hopeful beliefs about the possibilities for good in this life and for the world after this one.
- Read scripture and other spiritual books. Many excellent books about grief are written by holy people who consider the nature of our spirits and what spirit needs to thrive in difficult times like grief.
- Seek wisdom outside your spiritual tradition, but be wary of making a new spiritual "home" too quickly. Typically, while grieving we are advised to wait awhile before making major changes of any kind.
- Hold (or say) the rosary or another spiritual object that reminds you of God as you perceive God to be.
- Create a prayer flag to hang on your wall. Prayer flags are a series of three or four squares on which hand-drawn pictures or other depictions signify the relationship you have to your loved ones or to other important spiritual relationships.

- Imagine the protection of a guardian angel looking over your life on Earth. Give thanks for this angel's vigilance.
- Pray that your loved one is looking after you from the next world.
- Practice forgiveness in every possible area of your life. Ask forgiveness of others.

Listening for answers with meditation

Using *Bead Blessing* mourning beads or some other object, sit or lay in a relaxed meditative pose that you can comfortably hold. It does not have to be a traditional yoga pose, although you can use such a pose if you would like. Finger a different bead for a new line of the mantra, use each bead to count how many total mantras you have said, or simply cradle and feel the beads for their healing comfort. Remember to breathe deeply in and out as you say a mantra. Here are some mantras you can use:

Through God

Through God's grace, we love;
In grief and loss, love still abides;
God's grace has new dimensions.

The Light of God

The Light of God surrounds you.
The Love of God enfolds you.

The Presence of God watches over you.
The Power of God protects you.
Wherever you are, God is.

I Love

I have loved deeply.
I love completely.
I will continue to love richly.

Incredibly Loveable[9]

You are incredibly loveable.
You have always been incredibly loveable.
You always will be incredibly loveable.
Your true nature is love.

This last mantra is especially helpful to say at least five times very slowly. It may bring tears because it connects us to the essence of pure Love. Change the second person "you" to first person "I" to connect with yourself. Change it to a name to connect with the beloved deceased. This mantra also is wonderful for blessing people around us if we're feeling disconnected from the world. Look at different people and silently say one line to each. On a deeply spiritual level, this mantra allows us to connect with the essence of those people as loveable rather than as strangers.

What other mourning activities can address your spirit?

[9] This mantra was developed by Skip Ellis, LCSW and Marilyn Ellis, LCSW for their psychotherapy practice.

Chapter 5

Mourning with Our Bodies

Death is a deep wound to our hearts and spirits. Mourning is the process of healing that wound. However, like a physical wound, death can leave scars. If the wound was deep-rooted because our loss was profound, the scar tissue also will be deep. Just like a physical scar reveals changes in the skin and possibly numbness because of damaged nerves, we also will be changed with grief.

Think of physical scars as maps of our lives. Each scar tells a story of our rich personal histories. Each scar speaks of a wound that, while painful, might have occurred in a humorous, frightening, or even a tragic context. In a way, these scars are beautiful because they are such an intimate part of our lives. Maybe this sounds a little crazy; I used to think of my scars as supremely ugly. More recently, though, I have begun to understand that my scars map the depths of my life. They reveal that I have lived fully even when the living has been hard—and maybe even because the living has been hard.

Similarly, our grief scars are intimately a part of us, and it's all right to acknowledge that a part of our grief always will be there. You'll always miss your loved one as you continue your life, which is why other people's comments about "getting over it" are extremely annoying, even hurtful. Acknowledging the reality of grief is a part of integrating grief into our lives—it's part of your personal shell stone. Although we live in a culture that attempts to wipe away all wrinkles and unsightly body parts, being healthy means accepting our physical *and* grief scars as natural, normal, and necessary to being human.

Just as our bodies have scars that expose our past wounds, we can use our bodies to mourn and to integrate our grief into our lives. Bodywork often involves doing or making something with our hands, but it also can involve such different activities as eating, travelling, vocalizing, and dancing.

> *We find a place for what we lose. Although we know that after such a loss the acute stage of mourning will subside, we also know that we shall remain inconsolable and will never find a substitute. No matter what may fill the gap, even if it be filled completely, it nevertheless remains something else.* Sigmund Freud

Using the Grieving Body

Seeing the Doctor

> **If you have any of the following symptoms while you are grieving, seek immediate medical attention!**
>
> - Chest pain
> - Arm pain
> - Jaw pain
> - Shortness of breath
> - Suicidal thoughts

Our bodies take a severe hit in grief. Of course, our bodies don't operate separately from our minds and spirits, but they do manifest the signs of grief physically. Sometimes the body is exhausted and unable to get off the sofa or out of bed without a great deal of determination. The lower energy levels that we have in grief can leave the body without reserves. It can feel like having the flu with the symptoms of headache, sore muscles, and lethargy all combined to keep us feeling down.

In contrast, some people have bodies that won't accept slowing down as a way to deal with grief. These people, like me, can't sleep well and get up in the early hours to walk the house, attempt to read, or surf the Internet. As the body connects with the mind, which signals that there's no way to get through the next day without enough rest, one's body still may refuse to let go of tension and to sleep. In this way, the body can overpower the mind and spirit in favor of remaining awake. Exhaustion can lead to deep circles under the eyes and possible illness.

The number one mourning activity that involves the body is to go to a physician—usually an internist or primary care doctor—that we know and trust (or to find one if necessary). Talking to our doctors about our loss, bereavement, and physical symptoms is a positive mourning step toward recovering. This simple act—which can be hard to do given the heaviness of grief—signals that we have set an intention to heal. It means that we have an expectation of making it through the grief and back to the world of the living.

What do doctors need to know?

- Who died, when the death occurred, and the relationship we had with this person
- Physical symptoms that may have changed with the grief
    - Sleep quality and amount
    - Eating habits
    - Exercise routines
    - Alcohol and recreational drug use
    - Prescription drug and supplement use
    - Crying quality and amount
    - Depression, anxiety, restlessness, or other symptoms
- What you believe about grief and mourning and your capacity to deal with this death
- What kind of support you want from the doctor

If you can't remember all of these things, which is natural in the time pressure of a short doctor's visit, write them down and either read the note aloud or give it to your doctor to read.

The doctor can counsel us about sleeping problems or any physical symptoms of grief. He or she can help by determining whether any physical issues are due to a bacterial infection, virus, or other organic problem that medication can help. When necessary, a doctor can help us find support groups, grief counselors, and other medical specialists. Perhaps most important, though, the doctor can be an objective observer who will see us more frequently during the early months of grief, which can help relieve any anxiety we might have regarding whether the physical symptoms are grief-related, organic, or both.

Please know that grief-related physical symptoms are normal. Many people get them precisely because of the body/mind/spirit connection that we have discussed. Having difficulty sleeping or eating well, over eating, getting frequent colds or sinus infections, feeling depressed, and the like are typical in bereaved people. What we need to do is to act on these symptoms in positive and honest ways. There's nothing to be ashamed of in these symptoms. In terms of our bodies, seeing the doctor is the first and most positive way to address the grief.

Enhancing Our Wellness

What else can you do to enhance your wellness when grieving? Here are some things that I have found helpful, but remember to follow your doctor's advice and to pay attention to your unique physical needs.

- Set a pattern for potentially restful sleep. Go to bed at a regular time each night.
    - Try not to watch television too late or to fall asleep by the television's noise as that same noise can disturb your ability to get to deeper levels of sleep.
    - Set a pleasant bell alarm or find another peaceful way to wake up in the morning.
    - Get rid of furniture that disturbs your rest. For example, if your spouse died in bed and you can't sleep peacefully in that bed anymore, buy a new mattress and rearrange the room if necessary.
- Eat some nutritious foods each day.

- If you typically don't care for vegetables, for example, add them a little at a time or have a bowl of soup. The body especially needs the vitamins that these foods provide. If you can't manage such foods, then talk to your doctor about drinking a high-quality supplemental protein drink.
- Avoid overeating. The Germans have a special word for the kind of overeating we do while grieving: *Kummerspeck*. This word literally means "grief bacon" or "emotional eating," which happens in all cultures. Remember that overdoing anything while grieving will have a negative impact on our bodies.
- Shop the edges of the grocery store: fruits, vegetables, fresh meats, and dairy products. Try to avoid the processed foods that come in boxes, bottles, and cans because their chemical ingredients can cause sluggishness during an already difficult time.
- If you are alone, it can be especially difficult to eat well. I know that I hate cooking just for myself, and I have heard many widows and widowers say that same thing. Make an effort to get at least one fully nutritious meal each day—even if you have to go to a local diner to get it—and snack healthfully the rest of the day on such food as fruit, fresh nuts, and cheese.
- Drink plenty of fresh water to stay hydrated, which will help with an overall healthy feeling.

Get some exercise or fresh air each day.

- When you suffer a new grief, it isn't the time to plan to run a marathon, especially if you don't already exercise regularly. However, it is possible to add some exercise to your day. Just moving about a little bit can help your body to cope with grief.
- Walk around the block twice, go up and down the stairs several times, join an aqua-size class, or ride a bike on an old trail.

  - On warm days, sit outside for a few minutes, and enjoy the sunshine. Just a few minutes in the sun can increase healthful vitamin D in the body.
  - Throw a ball to a dog or pick some weeds out of the garden. Mindless activity can clear up fuzzy thinking.
- Sit to breathe, pray, and meditate. See chapter 4 for the benefits of these activities.

Mourning with Our Hands

Crafts for Mourners

When we use our hands to make or build something, we engage our bodies in the grief. Even if our bodies feel tired or restless, it's possible to bring about some level of calm by using the body in the act of creation. Simple craft making is a useful way to mourn physically because many crafts, once learned, provide rote activity and enable us to think about the one that the craft is designed to commemorate. It also allows us to focus on our grief and how it's changing our lives by ripples or tsunamis. The thinking that occurs in the background of the craft making can enable us to move through grief's sticking points.

For example, one craft that enables such thinking is to make a collage from various materials like construction paper, fabric, ribbon, foam stickers, and magazine photographs. Because younger children also like to cut, paste, and manipulate images, this activity is helpful to do with family members.

- Select a theme for the collage like one of the following:
  - My life with my beloved,
  - What my life is like without my beloved,
  - Where I think my beloved is right now,
  - What I would like to do in the next year,
  - What grief looks like, or
  - What hope looks like.
- While you select and use the materials to create your collage, your mind may be thinking about your loved one and his or

her past and continuing place in your life. If you're making this collage with other people, feel free to talk with them about what you're thinking.

- When you're finished, explain the collage to someone: *What is your message? What pictures or images symbolize your thoughts, ideas or goals? What does this collage help you understand about your grief? What possible next steps come to your mind for your mourning journey?*

A similarly helpful craft is to make a grave wreath or blanket. A grave blanket is a woven cover of evergreens and holiday rickrack and bows. It's designed to be staked to a grave in the winter months with the symbolic purpose of warming the beloved's grave. We can pay many dollars for a grave wreath at a florist shop or make it ourselves, which increases its value as a mourning activity.

Materials:

- Metal or plastic mesh (typically used to construct garden fences)
- Live evergreen branches or plastic branches/garland
- Holiday bows and decorative items
- Scissors or wire cutters
- Twist-ties for securing the decorations
- U-shaped wire garden stakes to secure the blankets to the ground

Cut the mesh to the size you prefer. The blanket can be as large or small as you want—to cover the entire grave or just a portion. Weave the evergreen through a piece of mesh (wire mesh for live cuttings and plastic for plastic garland). This process can take many cuttings or garland yards depending on how full you want the blanket to be. Use twist-ties to secure the decorations to the blanket. Take the finished blanket to the grave and secure it with the garden stakes.

Creating the grave blanket, Step 1

Creating the grave blanket, Step 2

The completed grave blanket

As with a collage, this craft can be constructed individually or by a few people. Weigh the value of being alone with handwork versus being in a situation where you can talk with others. One experience with making grave blankets in a pre-holiday grief workshop found a family of two parents and an adult child bonding over the blanket by talking about the deceased adult child. Apparently, the environment was safe, and the normally reserved father both helped with the craft and talked about his deceased daughter more freely than usual. Healing can occur in this highly symbolic and physical mourning activity.

Other craft-like activities that use our bodies include:

- *Herb pots.* Painting clay pots in colors that represent how you feel and planting a favorite herb or flower in the pot. Symbolically, this activity represents nurturing a new life for ourselves and our living loved ones.
- *Keepsake box construction from shoeboxes or other sturdy containers.* Cover with paper, paint, or objects to fit your mood. Use this box to keep sympathy cards or small linking objects that connect to your loved one. Symbolically, this activity represents the need to keep what's important from the past.
- *Mosaic.* Create something entirely new from a shattered pot or vase by gluing the broken and smashed pieces into a mosaic for hanging onto the wall or placing upon a table. Symbolically, this activity represents recreating our lives that have been shattered by grief.
- *Angel bears.* Find small stuffed bears (or other animals) from stores, valentine candy boxes, or yard sales. Make wings from lace or other fabric. Using hot glue, attach the wings and other decorations like bows and medals (holy medals, angels, doves, butterflies, dragonflies, or the like). Give the bears to other bereaved individuals in your family and among friends grieving your beloved. Symbolically, this activity represents finding and giving the good in your bereavement to others.

Making angel bears, Step 1

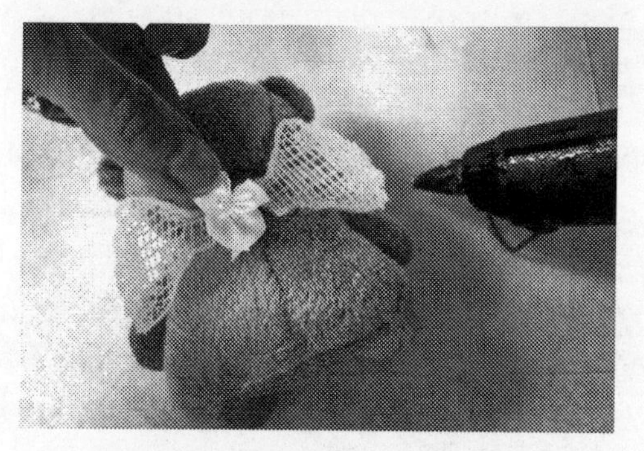

Making angel bears, Step 2

The completed angel bears

Art and Mourning

Beyond general craft projects, we can use the arts to mourn physically. We can paint, draw, sculpt, or sew, for example. These activities may require a little more skill if you want to make something to hang on the wall, but for most people—me included—experience and skill count less than the effort that has gone into the activity. In fact, after the activity, I may not look at the item again for a long time. For me, the finished creation often isn't as important as the time and thought I put into doing it. The mourning benefits for me are in the act of doing.

For example, anyone can use paints and paper to mourn physically. I'm someone who can't draw a dog that looks like anything other than a rat. My circles are ovals and my butterflies are like triangles. But, I can paint out my grief through a variety of paints—gouache, watercolor, oils, and tempera—and multiple colors. You can, too. Try writing the date on each piece to see how your grief changes over time.

One of my deceased brother's daughters is an artist. Virginia worked primarily in charcoal, pencil, and black pen for many years after George died. The people she drew were faceless and nameless. I think that each in some way represented part of her adolescent life without a father and struggle to relate to men. Then, when Kathy was dying, Virginia visited her several times in the hospital. One night, she returned home late and began painting in color. She worked through the night and created the picture shown below. This painting represents a release of some sort, a breaking of chains—whether Virginia's or my sister's chains, I don't know—and, particularly when viewed in color, it's an amazing example of mourning using one's body.[10]

[10] To see this painting in color, go to http://www.goodwordsforgrieving.com/what-grief-can-teach-us/

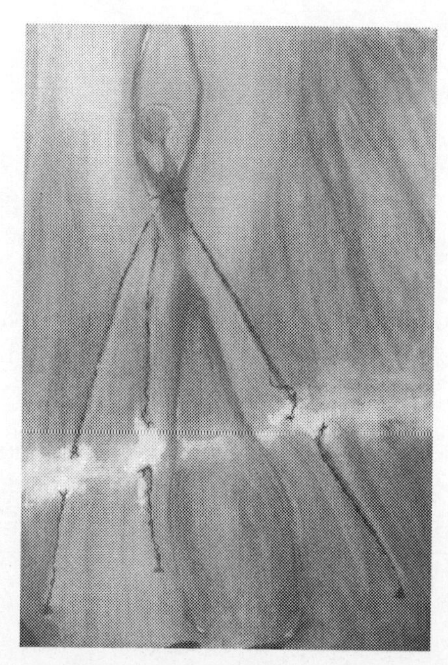

***Release into Life* by Virginia Lee Lengyel**

Sewing to Mourn

Sewing is another art with which I'm not gifted. My mother Daryl is, however, and she has created a number of sewn mourning articles:

- A sweatshirt quilt from my mother-in-law's favorite "kitty" sweatshirts for warming my father-in-law after her death
- Pillows for each of their children and grandchildren from the remaining sweatshirt kitty designs
- A pillow from my father's ties as a memento for his best friend
- A T-Shirt pillow from Dad's favorite shirt with which she sleeps.
- Memorial T-Shirt quilts for each of the grandchildren.

Part of the beauty of these articles is that Mom made them for other people and, in the process, mourned with her hands and sewing machine. Her gifts were physically useable, which means that the recipient could admire, touch, and hold them. Such items often are made of a loved one's clothes, which gives them a homey feel and familiar scent. They provide an emotional closeness from connecting with the deceased. All kinds of fabrics and parts of clothes can be used to develop this closeness: parts of old quilts to make new ones, flannel and cotton shirts, zippers, pockets, ties, baby blankets, and even jewelry like broaches and scout pins.

Books and Websites are available with patterns for sewing many wonderful mourning articles, but they have varying levels of difficulty.[11] If, like me, you aren't particularly skilled at sewing, you can have an experienced sewer make what you want or you can use one of these simple patterns that my mother has developed for mourning through sewing.

Hug Pillow

1. Lay out a clean T-Shirt or polo shirt on a hard surface. Make sure the top and bottom meet evenly.
2. Measure and mark the size pillow you would like. A 19" x 19" size provides a reasonable size pillow. The 19" x 19" size includes a 1" seam allowance.
3. Cut the T-Shirt to the marked square size. [If you want rounded corners, trace the edges of a small plate at each corner and cut to the rounded shape.]
4. Pin the fabric with right sides together.
5. Machine stitch all around the pillow, leaving a 5" opening at the bottom.
6. Trim the seams to ½".
7. Turn the pillow right side out.
8. Fill it will cotton batting without overstuffing. Make sure the corners are stuffed.
9. Hand stitch the opening closed with a whipstitch.

---

[11] See, for example, Shirley Botsford, *Daddy's Ties: A Project and Keepsake Book* (Radnor, PA: Chilton Book Co., 1994). See also Jane Davila and Linda Oehler Marx, *T-Shirt Quilts*. (The Country Quilter, 2004).

10. Hug as needed!

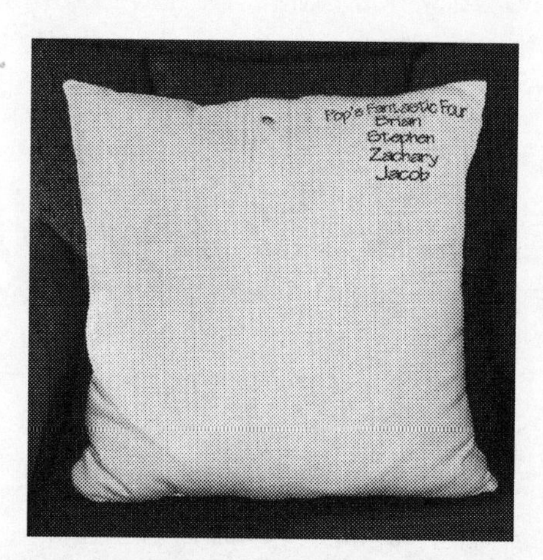

A T-Shirt hug pillow

Variation 1: Using a small T-Shirt, leave the entire shirt intact. Turn it inside out and stitch the neck, armholes, and most of the bottom, leaving about 5" opening for turning and stuffing. Trim the seams if needed. Turn it right side out, stuff, and whipstitch the bottom closed.

Variation 2: Following the directions above, cut the shirt into a circle using a large dinner plate or round platter as a guide. Sew the circle, leaving 5" open for stuffing and stitching. Trim the seams to ½".

Variation 3: Using a T-Shirt or polo shirt, follow most of the directions outlined above. However, use a 20" x 20" size rather than the smaller 19" x 19". Insert a pillow form that can be purchased at any sewing or craft store. Manipulate the corners of the pillow until they are filled. Whipstitch the bottom closed. Because of the pillow form, this pillow will be less malleable and may be more decorative than comfortable for hugging.

Like pillows, T-Shirt or sweat shirt quilts are easy to make even for non-quilters. Collect your loved one's favorite T-Shirts, sweatshirts, or even flannel shirts and slacks. Here is Daryl's easy pattern for a T-Shirt quilt for non-sewers. If you would like more information on how to plan and sew such a quilt, use the Internet to find additional patterns and video tutorials.

Memorial T-Shirt quilt, Step 1

Memorial T-Shirt quilt, Step 2

T-Shirt Quilt

1. Select, wash, and dry about 18 T-Shirts. The number of squares determines the size of the quilt.
2. Measure and cut the front and/or back of shirts (about 15" x 15"), depending on what images and designs you want in the quilt. Be sure that you have at least ½ inch seam allowance on all four sides of each piece. These pieces will become the top of the quilt. It is easiest if all your shirt squares are the same size, so be sure to measure the largest design first and cut accordingly.
3. On the backside of each T-Shirt piece, iron on a lightweight fusible interfacing (like Pellon™).
4. Arrange your squares in the design you desire for your quilt. You may need to rearrange a few times, or even take a break and come back to it.

5. Sew two pieces together by laying them face to face, stitching across the bottom. Press the seam open. Continue adding new pieces until achieving the length you want, which is probably about 6 T-Shirt squares for one row. Complete this process with all three sets of squares. [Variation: sew borders on each T-Shirt piece to separate the T-Shirts from each other.]
6. Sew the three strips of T-Shirt pieces together lengthwise: row 1 to row 2 and row 2 to row 3. Press (iron) all seams open. This is the front of the quilt.
7. When the top is finished, lay out the back of quilt, which will be a cotton-blend fabric with a pattern and color that enhances the appearance of the T-Shirts you have selected. To figure out how much fabric to buy, measure the fully sewn quilt top. Or, purchase 9 yards of 42 inches of fabric and cut it in half width wise. Lay the lengths of these two pieces together right sides facing. Stitch a seam down to the length to achieve a single piece of fabric of 4 ½ yards by about 80 inches. Press the seam open. This seam becomes the center of the back of the quilt.
8. Purchase a "low loft" batting in the amount that will cover the full quilt.
9. With the wrong side of the back facing up, place the batting on top of the back. To keep the batting from moving, use a spray adhesive like Quick Tack™
10. Lay the quilt top face up on the batting. The quilt now has three layers. Secure these layers with safety pins being careful to keep the quilt smooth and taut. Trim the back piece of fabric to match the quilt top.
11. Using embroidery floss or a heavy decorative cord and with a large-eye needle, tie the quilt together at 3-inch to 4-inch intervals using square knots. Tying the quilt connects and secures all three layers and eliminates the need to hand or machine-quilt the top (Variation: hand- or machine-quilt the top].
12. To finish the quilt, use 2 ½-inch binding, which can be purchased in the store. Or, on the straight grain, cut a 2 ½-inch strip of the fabric used for the quilt's backing. Pin the binding right side to the right side of the quilt top. On the top side of the quilt, machine stitch this binding through all three layers with a ¼-inch seam.

13. Turn the binding to the back of the quilt, enclosing the quilt's raw edge, and turning under at least another ¼ inch of the binding's raw edge. Pin the binding to the fabric. Either machine- or hand-stitch the binding to the back edges of the quilt.

Memorial T-Shirt wall quilt

<u>Variation 1: T-Shirt Quilt Wall Hanging:</u>

1. Choose the shirts you want to use in your wall-hanging. It is ideal to choose a number of shirts that will fit together as a whole (4, 6, or 9 to make a square or rectangle).
2. Follow Step 2, above.
3. Follow Step 3, above.
4. Follow Step 4, above.
5. Lay the first 2 squares face to face, and sew on the side you want them connected. If desired, add another square to this row. Repeat for each row.
6. Follow Step 6, above.
7. If you are choosing to add a border to the quilt:
    a. Choose a fabric that enhances the shirts or perhaps is a theme that the person you are memorializing would have enjoyed (for example, their favorite animal, sports team, or color)
    b. Measure how long the quilt front is, then add 3 1/2 inches. Cut 4 strips of fabric to this length, each 3 1/2 inches wide.

   c. Line up one strip with the top left corner of the quilt; sew it face to face like with the shirt rows. The extra 3 1/2 in. will hang off the right side.
   d. Take your next strip and fit it to the right side of the quilt, sew face to face again, but also connect it to the 3 1/2 in. that is hanging off from the previous step.
   e. Repeat for the last 2 sides.
   f. For more detailed instructions, or to watch a tutorial don't be afraid to look this up online.

7. Choose a fabric for the back of your quilt. Because this is a wall hanging it can be anything you choose. Measure your quilt front to know how much you will need. Since this is a wall hanging you don't need to use any batting or fill.
8. Lay the quilt front on top of the backing fabric so that it is pattern to pattern and both wrong sides are facing out. Cut the backing so that it is the same size as the front. Pin pieces together, leaving about a 3-to-4-inch hole to turn the quilt.
9. Sew pieces together making sure to leave the turn-hole open. Turn right-side out when finished.
10. Press all sides, including the turned hole; then, hand-sew the hole closed.
11. Either hand or machine-quilt the top. Because this is a wall hanging and not for use, it isn't necessary to do a lot of quilting since. Stitching around the shirt squares and the border is sufficient, but feel free to do more if desired.
12. Hand sew a fabric casing to the back of the quilt near the top (about 2 inches wide and as long as the quilt), leaving the ends open. Choose a decorative curtain rod or a dowel rod with a decorative cord to hang the quilt.

Mourning with the Whole Body

We can use our entire bodies for mourning. Although it might sound odd given our grief, we can work out some of our feelings through entire body engagement. Wailing and keening are two body-intensive mourning activities that we already have discussed. Here are some other activities that engage our bodies in the mourning process.

- *Dance*. Go with a family member to a square dance. Learn to swing or ballroom dance. Join a Zumba class, the new Latin-based rage in dance exercise. The benefits of being with people—even if you don't talk to them individually—and of sweating, moving, and feeling music does wonders for a body that is dealing with exhausting grief. Such primal movement can lead to a good night's sleep. It's okay if you give dancing a try and find that one type of dance reminds you too much of your beloved deceased. In that case, try again with another kind of dance or a different full body activity like hula hooping.

- *Sing*. Whenever I have been newly bereaved, I actually can't sing. My heart feels so much in my throat that it's all I can do to stop tears. Any attempt at singing leads to a choking sensation. In fact, I can barely tolerate being in church and hearing traditional hymns. So, when I suggest singing, I know how hard this activity can be. Here are some thoughts: Join a choir, belt out sad or snazzy songs to the radio, or just sing to yourself *a cappella*. Singing can lead to helpful tears, but it also can defy tears by raising your mood. Using the voice is a way to move energy, which expresses feelings; our voices move energy up and out of the body, opening new space inside for love. In a way, singing has many of the effects of a good cry or screaming out feelings, but it's gentler.

- *Exercise*. Moving the body helps with grief. Walking, running, swimming, playing tennis, golfing, biking, or dancing are ways to get your body moving. However, be sure to respect your body's need for rest and exercise safely, within your range of ability and aerobic fitness. If you haven't been an avid exerciser until now, forget planning a marathon run at this point. Set small, manageable goals. Stretch before and after exercise. Consider yoga, tai chi, or another gentle, breathing-based exercise if your body aches with grief. Swimming and water-based exercise classes also can be helpful.

- *Explore.* Travel is something we might not feel much like doing right after a death of a loved one. Exploration has a different appeal for different people, though. Some people want to get away from their homes that now seem empty or foreign. Others can't bear leaving the house even for work. Travel might be an activity to save for later in the mourning journey. Travelling can be a part of healthy mourning in several ways. If you plan to go to a destination that you and your loved one had planned to visit and didn't have the chance, then the travel can complete a mutual goal with healing satisfaction. During the trip, you'll undoubtedly converse with your deceased loved one—sharing your grief and new discoveries. This kind of activity helps to integrate the death into your new life. Similarly, travelling to a new destination without your loved one—but perhaps with other bereaved individuals—can help to support a new self-identity during this challenging time.

- *Touch.* Physical touch is important. Get a hand, foot, or full-body massage. Physically, we miss hugs and touch from our beloved. Human bodies have a strong, biologically based need for touch. Studies have shown that babies raised in an orphanage without frequent cuddling and holding do not thrive and may not survive; many die. It's crucial, then, to find healthy ways to get this need for touch met. Partners dancing (for example, square, swing, and ballroom styles) provide a safe way to connect physically with our hands and arms. Some people might benefit from contact sports like football, soccer, and basketball. Volunteering to hold premature babies or to play with animals at a local animal shelter can help as well. Touch reconnects us to the world when we most feel disconnected.

- *Consider body art.* You may crave or envision a permanent image of your loved one. Consider whether a tattoo would be right for you. While it isn't unusual for people to honor their loved ones with a tattoo, family members may object or caution about using the body as a mourning canvas. Body art is a highly personal decision. Because a tattoo is a fairly permanent mark of mourning, it's a decision worth making over time rather than suddenly upon the loved one's death.

Other Physical Mourning Activities

- Develop a new hobby (for example, playing the harmonica, guitar, or piano; learning an art form like brush painting; taking up archery, horseback riding, or gardening).
- Build (or design) a memorial fountain or a dedicated bench in a public place so that others can enjoy your memory of the beloved.
- Rest (but get out of bed at a regular time each day, watching for depression).
- Eat something in memory of the deceased. Much like we share a cake on a birthday or anniversary, ritual eating can help with mourning. Slurp some oysters in honor of an oyster lover.
- Make a toast—an age-old act—silently or aloud. Fill a cup for the dead, and pour it onto the grave or into the ground; this is called a libation. These acts honor our loved ones and us, and they can be remarkably soothing.
- Get hugs—lots of them. When we are deprived of physical hugs and other human touch, we can decline emotionally and spiritually. If hugs are not available, pay for a full-body massage or hands, foot, and/or facial massage. Touch is that important!
- Indulge in a picnic or outdoor concert.
- Build a memorial garden, playground, or park.
- Plant a tree with a dedication stone.
- Name a boat in honor of the beloved.

> *One special kind of memorial is an Angel of Hope memorial garden. These gardens, commissioned and paid for by local communities of bereaved parents, are special places to honor the lives of their deceased children. I have seen this lovely angel hold up toward heaven hundreds of long-stemmed roses offered by bereaved parents, grandparents, and siblings. Richard Paul Evans, author of* The Christmas Box, *designed this angel statue. See this photograph of the porcelain figurine and go to http://www.richardpaulevans.com/angel-statues for more information.*

***Angel of Hope* statue**

Wall memorials for *Angel of Hope*

Finally, be gentle with yourself. Drink plenty of water. Otherwise, eat and drink nutritiously, but allow yourself some comfort foods and comfort activities. An occasional day with macaroni and cheese and hot chocolate while watching a movie in a bathrobe can be an appropriate way to use our bodies at certain times of grief.

What other mourning activities can address or use your body?

Chapter 6

Mourning with Our Minds

Bereaved people often experience cognitive difficulties when grieving. Many people say that they have brain fog causing them not to remember times, dates, or appointments. Some express not being able to recall words, manipulate numbers, or complete a task without first moving on to other tasks. I commonly hear from the bereaved that a day begun with making the bed can end with an unmade bed and a multitude of other started-but-unfinished tasks. When acutely in grief, my mother cannot read, others cannot concentrate on a movie, and I cannot express myself well verbally.

These mental challenges are real, and they're quite common with grief. Not only does grief disrupt our thinking, but grief-based physical behaviors like sleeplessness, poor nutrition, and lack of adequate hydration also make cognitive difficulties worse.

> *Give sorrow words; the grief that does not speak whispers the o'er-fraught heart and bids it break.* William Shakespeare
>
> *There is no grief like the grief that does not speak.* Henry Wadsworth Longfellow

As both Shakespeare and Longfellow say so beautifully, the heart feels grief all the more intensely when we cannot express it in words. Yet, the grief itself works against expression—leaving it to us to consciously use our minds to make the words emerge.

Using the Mind to Create Possibility

To mourn in the cognitive realm, we may need our will power more than ever. That's because thinking can be difficult, and thinking is necessary to use words with our grief.

Expressing Intention

A beginning step is to set the conscious intention to heal from the grief. Remember that the idea is not to "get over" grief but to integrate it into our lives—the way a shell stone encapsulates a shell or coquina cements to other shells.

It can be helpful to have a mantra or statement that consciously expresses positive intention. *Expressing* clear intentions is a first step to making them real. Here are some possibilities:

- I choose to HOPE for a less painful life without my beloved.
- Life will be better again.
- It is good to be alive.
- I can do what is necessary to move through my grief.
- I know when and how to ask for help.
- To the degree that it's possible, I will ____________. *Fill in the blank with what you will do:*
    - express my grief through active mourning
    - forgive those who have hurt me
    - find new meaning in my life
    - accept my beloved's death and incorporate it into my life
    - help my family through grief
- I can do it.
- I must take care of myself before I can help others.

Notice that all of these are positive statements of what we can do. They don't express any sense of hopelessness or helplessness. Mourning emotionally, as discussed in chapter 3, will help to express those entirely natural but less hope-filled feelings.

Additionally, we can use *Bead Blessing*s or a linking object to connect the expressed intention to a physical object—a way to cement the thought just like the shell is encased in the shell stone. The more often we repeat these intentions, the clearer they become in our minds and the more we can discover mourning actions to bring the intention to fruition.

Another way to express an intention to heal is to figure out what can be corrected in this current life without the loved one and to accept what cannot be fixed. This mental activity can help when we torment ourselves with "if only" thoughts.

- *If only* I had slept on the couch instead of in the bedroom, she would not have died alone.
- *If only* I had come as soon as the call came, I would have been there for him.
- *If only* I had eaten dinner with him that night instead of going to the gym, I could have saved him.
- *If only* I had known how to give her enough pain medicine, she would not have needed to return to the hospital—where she died.

With "if only" thinking, we bereaved imagine ourselves to be perpetrators who have failed to do something that—in our fantasy thoughts—would have saved the beloved from pain, death, or dying without us.

When Kathy died, I had those thoughts, too. Instead of immediately getting into the car when I got the call that she was actively dying, I had just finished a vigorous walk. I took a shower and encouraged my husband to take one, too. We missed her last breath by approximately the ten minutes of those showers. I felt guilty and angry with myself for a long time. It's a good idea to explore these thoughts as a part of mourning. Doing so can help us realize what we genuinely are responsible for doing or not doing versus those actions for which we have no responsibility.

To work with my feelings, I needed to connect with what I thought my "being there" would have done. I couldn't have stopped my sister from dying. My mother and brother and her husband already were there, so she didn't die alone. She was unconscious, so she probably didn't know whether I was there or not. *What was my guilt and anger about?* I realized that on a visceral level, I was angry that I couldn't save my sister, period. Being there wouldn't have helped. Nothing I could do would have saved her from dying when she did.

Here's an exercise that can help when "if only" thoughts arise. The exercise involves writing out the possible results of an "if only" moment.

1. *Write about the wish:* "If only I had ________, then ________ would not have happened."
2. *Write about the "unfixable":* "I tried everything in my power to ________."
3. *Write about what you can or cannot control:* "I can fix ________ about this situation, but I can't fix ________ about this situation."
4. *Write about the reality of the wish:* "Even if I had ________, ________ would have happened. I had control over ________ and not over ________."

In effect, the exercise helps us to understand cognitively that we can't always have control and that an out-of-control situation makes us feel powerless. Sometimes, we need to get those facts clear in our minds in order to let go of the "if only" thoughts. Letting go is one mourning step toward intentional healing.

Expressing Love Verbally

A eulogy is a significant way to express love for the deceased. A eulogy is a speech that praises and blesses the loved one, and in the process of doing so, it honors our relationship with him or her. Typically, it is delivered at a funeral or a memorial ceremony or other gathering of the bereaved. Sometimes more than one person will talk about, or eulogize, the deceased although in some settings only one person will be offered this opportunity.

The word *eulogy*, which comes from Greek, literally means "good words." Eulogies essentially give voice to our losses. Writing, delivering, or listening to a eulogy is a mourning activity that involves the conscious mind. Because there's a purpose (to praise and bless the deceased), an audience (the bereaved), and a special occasion (the ceremony or gathering), a eulogy is a unique opportunity to share our relationship with the deceased formally. By writing, rewriting, and talking about our loved ones, we begin to heal the grief created by death.

In the eulogy, we praise the essence of the deceased—who she really was in terms of her best qualities and how he lived the virtues that he valued. This person's character and relationships are the building blocks of a good eulogy—not one's job, career, or hobbies. People who can listen to or read the eulogy receive help in processing their losses and in experiencing healthy grief. This speech encourages a communal sharing of the grief among all who are present. It supports all of the bereaved, but especially the family, as they begin to awaken from the shock of the death. Often, people will want to reread the well-written eulogy because of the comfort it offers.

To write a eulogy, we look at three central things about the deceased. First, we gather a few factual details. Then, we talk with loved ones about some short biographical stories that tell something special about the deceased. Finally—and most importantly—we consider this person's finest character qualities in terms of values, virtues, and noble deeds in life. *Good Words: Memorializing Through a Eulogy*[12] walks readers through the questioning, writing, rewriting, and delivery processes. It also provides ample examples and explains various digital modes for sharing the eulogy electronically.

Using *Good Words: Memorializing Through a Eulogy*, Kathleen Reinhard, a bereaved sister of a fallen U.S. Marine, developed the following eulogy that honors her precious brother:

---

[12] *Good Words: Memorializing Through a Eulogy* is available in hardbound, paperback, and e-book forms with WestBow Press and through various bookselling outlets. It also is available as isolated chapters in booklet form at www.goodwordsforgrieving.com and amazon.com.

Eulogizing a Loved One

Please let me start by saying that my parents and I thank you for being here with us.

We are gathered here today to celebrate the life of my brother, Kevin James R.

Many of you knew my brother in some capacity; as a family member, co-worker, teammate, classmate, and friend. Others gathered here did not know my brother personally; however, his gifts of serving our country and of laying down his own life so that our lives could be safer and of a better quality have brought you here today.

Those of you who knew my brother, know that he was a man of many stories. Some of Kevin's stories were true, and some of them were expanded upon by his creative genius. He was a "the fish was this big" kind of guy. I have never been very good at creating elaborate stories; but the kind of life my brother lived needs no elaboration to capture an audience. The truth, of the way he lived his life, is fascinating enough.

From his early childhood, Kevin was the sort of person who always thought of others and placed his concern for others above himself. He was not just respectful or gentle, Kevin was chivalrous; a White Knight, from childhood to manhood, and in death.

At a very young age Kevin looked out for and loved everyone and everything – right down to our pet goldfish. Each night he would dip his hand into the fish tank, take out the fish and kiss the fish good night. He would pet the fish and tell it sweet dreams, and tell it that he loved it before putting it back in the tank. Little did he know that he was killing the fish with his kindness; Mom and Dad replaced that fish just about every other week.

As a little boy, when he went to the bank with one of my parents, he would always take a lollipop for himself and never failed to ask for another… one for his Sissy. My brother never once thought only of himself; even as a little boy. He did not take the lollipop for himself; he always brought it home and was so excited to give it to me.

Later on, around 5th or 6th grade, Kevin ran track. During his first big run, at Warrinako Park, Kevin was lapping his competition. However, when he noticed that one of his teammates was having difficulty keeping up with the rest, Kevin jogged in place until the other child caught up to him, and shouted words of encouragement the entire time. Parents and coaches were yelling at Kevin to keep running, but it was more important to him that he made sure his teammate finished the race, than for himself to finish first.

As Kevin grew into a man his chivalrousness did not falter. Kevin assisted my Aunt Mary Beth in caring for our Grandmother as she grew older. Just as our Grandmother helped raise us, Kevin helped drive her to appointments, injected her with her insulin, and helped out around the house. Aunt Mary Beth especially appreciated utilizing his height to clean the gutters. While many other grandsons or nephews would take money for these services, Kevin never took a cent.

Kevin's generosity was known to many, even though he never spoke of it himself. Kevin was not the kind of person who would gloat about the things he did for others. He did them quietly and without hesitation. In his younger years, my brother often used me as a venue for generosity towards others – namely having me buy pizzas for he and his friends with the promise of paying me back (although he never did). I guess you could say we were both generous people.

As the story goes, an indelible impression was left on more than just the recipient of my brother's unspoken generosity the night that he met one of his college friends. While out with friends, Kevin was introduced to, and spent a good deal of time speaking with, one young man in particular. Kevin LOVED cars and the two bonded over their passion for horsepower. However, the young man was having difficulty making his car payments… and was rather depressed that evening. Kevin left that night, and later on the next day a phone call was made by the young man. Someone had left him $200 so that he could make his next car payment and keep his vehicle. That someone was my brother.

It goes without saying that Kevin simply left an envelope of cash, designating it for the car payment, and did so without ever expecting a thank you, without expecting to be paid back, and in fact Kevin would have turned the money down if payment back had been attempted. Kevin was self-less in his generosity.

However, Kevin's generosity and thoughtfulness was not limited to monetary needs. In high school Kevin developed a very close bond with his freshman religion teacher. The man became Kevin's friend and mentor. Every year, since 2005, Kevin made sure to never forget his mentor's birthday. While my brother was in high school and college he made a birthday cake and brought it into school. When Kevin joined the Marine Corps, he called home to make sure that Mom or I had made and delivered the birthday cake on time.

What everyone who ever met my brother knew about him was his sense of humor. Kevin would do just about anything to put a smile on someone's face. He knew how to pick you up when you were down – even if you fought him while he was doing it.

When he was in high school, Kevin developed this very particular way of reading his birthday cards that would set the family rolling in laughter. I cannot begin to explain to you, or even try to mimic the way he did it. Things like that came naturally to him. He even developed a knack for picking up a spoon at the table and saying "look Sissy… it's a spoon." Usually this would set me off into a fit of laughter that ended with a whole lot of snorting laughter on my end and giggling on his. No one but my brother could make someone laugh that much over a simple spoon.

My parents, as many parents often do, sometimes wonder whether or not they did a good job raising their children. Wondering whether or not they were involved in their children's lives enough, wondering whether or not they spent enough time with their children when they were young. In situations such as this, no parent could ever believe that they spent enough time with their son.

However, what my parents may not understand is that my brother understood and appreciated all of the sacrifices they made on our behalves. Kevin knew that when Dad worked overtime it was because he wanted a better life, a better education, and a better future for his son. Dad's overtime enabled Kevin to attend St. Joe's High School…a school that my father dreamed of going to, and that provided my brother with the best years of his life. Dad, Kevin could have never enjoyed his teenage years without your sacrifice…and the time he did spend with you on days off became more precious to him because of it.

Our mother often wonders whether or not she was a good parent… if she provided Kevin with the quality of life that he should have had. Mom, Kevin lived his life like he was living a dream. He loved his family dearly…which is why he constantly spoke to me and to his friends about how he could not wait to come home to us. What he held onto during each deployment was coming home and spending time with his family. If you and Dad had not done a good job raising Kevin, he could not have been as loved as he is.

My brother and I were very close… often inseparable as children and teens, fighting here and there in college, and finally coming to learn and understand our differences and love each other because of them. No matter what our feelings for each other were at the time, we always stood up for and looked out for one another. One example, out of a countless many, was when I was unable to attend my junior prom, because I did not have a date. Kevin took me out. Instead of staying in my room, miserable that my friends were out for the night and I was stuck at home, Kevin made sure that I got dressed up and took me to a battle of the bands instead. I do not think I could have had anywhere near as much fun at my junior prom than I did that night with my brother.

It is because of the love and commitment we shared towards each other that we made a very special promise. If anything should happen to either one of us, the one who has been left behind would not leave the other's side. However, I do not now think that my brother has left me behind. I firmly believe that he is simply waiting for me… for each of us… that Kevin has gone to God before me, has asked for a lollipop for his Sissy, and is waiting patiently for my time to join him so he may give it to me. That he is jogging in place in this race we call life, shouting encouragements to each of you—to live your lives as fully as

> he did, to love as much as he loved, and that he is waiting for you to join him in heaven when your time comes.
>
> Do not think of this as a last farewell...think of this as the warmest welcome home my brother could have. We are not burying my brother today. Kevin lives on in each and every one of us; in our memories, in our love for him, and in the little pieces of himself that he imparted in each of us without our ever knowing it.

Remember that a eulogy can be written and shared anytime—*even after the funeral or memorial ceremony*. Sometimes, time gives perspective that makes a stronger eulogy. Eulogies can be shared after the fact:

- On personal Websites and Webpages offered by the funeral home
- Through email, grief-based discussion forums, and social networking sites like Facebook
- With audio/video media on free video forums like YouTube

Using the Mind to Understand Grief

Just as we can use our minds to create positive thoughts and hope, we can use our minds to understand the nature of our particular grief.

Reading about Grief

Reading books about other people's grief can help us to understand more about our own experiences. Literally thousands of books about grief have been written, and some are better than others are, so it's good to be discriminating about what we read. The books include, among other types:

- Psychological, spiritual, or heart-based explanations of grief
- Self-help for moving through grief written for various people (for example, parents, children, siblings, and friends)
- Stories of other people's grief intended to show us that we aren't alone
- Novels about grief that bring out both the poignant and humorous aspects of death

- Children's fiction about grief
- Spiritual and supernatural tales of life after death

Additionally, the Internet also includes books, blogs (Web-based personal journals), Websites, Web-based discussion forums, and other media regarding grief and mourning.

Any of these various kinds of publications can be helpful, but it's good to be discerning. There's no sense in reading materials that cause guilt or overwhelming feelings of sadness. It's okay to put such reading away for the time being.

For example, some people find support and help in Web-based discussion forums where people share advice and chat anonymously about their experiences of grief. However, without a thoughtful moderator, such forums easily can devolve into negativity and hopelessness that suck the participants in. It's essential to leave any forum or reading opportunity that creates or oozes guilt, hopelessness, or helplessness because these emotions aren't helpful for healthy mourning. In fact, walk away from any activity that causes you to remain stuck in grief.

Understandably, some bereaved people have cognitive difficulties reading, as we discussed earlier. However, it can be helpful to try to read about the illness or cause of death, particularly if it was sudden. Such reading can help us to let go of some of the "if only" talk and guilt involved in not having been able to save our loved ones from death. If reading is too difficult mentally right now, try getting the book in an audio version or ask a close friend or family member to read it to you in short chunks. Then, talking with someone about what was read can be helpful in sorting out the information.

Intellectually, it seems important to remember that whatever the cause of death—no matter how tragic and apparently unnecessary—*all of us will die*. That's the nature of human life. When we're mourning in the cognitive sphere, it's helpful to keep in mind that death isn't an elective in this school called life. Despite the fact that death catches us unaware and has serious consequences for everyone involved, often it can't be prevented. And, if it is prevented, the reprieve is temporary. Of course,

I don't mean that we shouldn't grieve, but only that we can choose to balance our natural grief with the perspective that death also is natural.

Some of my favorite books about grief—each written by people who understood grief intimately—include the following:

- Joan Didion's *A Year of Magical Thinking* (a memoir regarding the author's unexpected husband's death) and *Blue Nights* (a memoir regarding Didion's daughter's untimely death shortly after her husband's death)
- C. S. Lewis's *A Grief Observed* (a much beloved memoir regarding the author's grief as a widower)
- Alan Wolfelt's *Understanding Your Grief: Ten Essential Touchstones* (a non-fiction book written to help people walk through grief; there are variations of the book available specific to suicide, for example)
- Elisabeth Kübler-Ross and David Kessler's *On Grief and Grieving: Finding the Meaning of Grief Through the Five Stages of Loss* (a non-fiction work that details Kübler-Ross's understanding of her life as she was dying and provides her final understanding of grief)
- Anne Enright's *The Gathering* (a novel about nine siblings returning home to Ireland to attend their brother's wake)
- Lolly Winston's *Good Grief* (a novel about a widow's grief that offers readers both tears and laughter)

Writing about Grief

As a writer, I naturally see many ways to write about our grief. Research shows that writing is a uniquely helpful way to think about the nature of death and grief. More than conscious thinking alone, however, the physical act of writing can help us to ruminate subconsciously about the death and our grief, which provides the unconscious mind ways to integrate the death into our lives.

Letters

Writing letters can be a powerful way of talking directly to the deceased. No one else needs to see the letter, and you can be completely honest because of that. Letter writing for mourning can be accomplished on the computer or by hand. Handwriting does provide a slower, more intimate pace and approach to the communication. To give the letter the gravity it deserves, use nice stationary and a pen or pencil that you especially like.

Write letters of love, hate, and/or ambivalence. Express pain, sorrow, pleasure, and joy. Explain your despair and lay bare your heart. Keep the letter, burn it, tear it up, tuck it in a wailing wall, or even ask a good friend to mail it back to you in six months. In your letter, tell your beloved about something that is difficult to discuss. You may want to write multiple letters over time; although some grief workshops might suggest otherwise, writing one letter and letting it go won't "cure" all grief. It's merely one step of many possible mourning activities. Here are some example themes and opening prompts:

- *Let me tell you what life has been like since you died....*
- *This is what my day-to-day life is like....*
- *I wish you were here to do....*
- *What I miss most about you is.....*
- *You'll laugh when you hear what happened yesterday....*
- *Did you know that.....?*
- *On the day that you were born....*
- *On the day that you died....*
- *These are things I wish I had said to you earlier....*

Journals

Like letters, journal writing can use our minds purposefully toward mourning. Some people don't like to journal, and that's okay. However, it might be helpful to try out journaling in grief because this experience is different from journaling everyday life. In my experience, journaling through a momentous occasion like death and grief or significant life transitions like illness, job changes, marriage, or divorce can illuminate some of our most and least helpful behaviors. Some of these behaviors are ones that we learned early in childhood and don't serve well in the current phase of life. Raising our behaviors from the subconscious to the conscious mind can influence our mourning significantly.

Like letter writing, journaling can occur in any typed space using a computer, tablet, even a smart phone, or by hand. Journaling even can be done by speaking into some of these devices. When journaling by hand, try using a journal that "speaks" to your frame of mind in terms of your current grief or your intention and hope for integrating that grief. I have known the bereaved to look for more than an hour at the many beautiful journals available at a local bookstore—searching for just the right one. Because of the uniqueness of grief, a journal that you choose may suite your mourning work better than one someone else picks out for you. Similarly, select a pencil or pen for the way it feels and writes. Writing is a sensory activity as well as a mentally focused one, and the kinds of writing that you'll do deserves the best that you can find or afford.

Writing and journaling

The following are some journaling exercises that enable us to experience the entire emotional spectrum. They enable us to risk feeling the emotions that we need not keep inside any longer.

- *Write about death.* Where were you when your beloved died? What did you experience? What did you think about? What has life been like without him or her?
- *Write a "call and response."* Open a journal.
    - On the left page, write an entry to your loved one. What do you miss most about him or her? What have you learned about life and love?
    - On the right page, allow your loved one's voice to write back to you and respond to your lament. Imagine that your

beloved is sitting on your shoulder and whispering in your ear. What is he or she saying?

- If you are experiencing a more complicated grief because of unmourned or incompletely mourned losses, *write a call and response journal entry for each beloved deceased person.* Doing so will help you to focus on healing your heart around your most recently deceased loved one's death.

These journaling exercises help us to understand our expectations. The Rolling Stones taught us that life does not always give us what we want, but it does tend to give us what we need. [13]

- *Write about your expectations of life.* We bring to life a series of expectations that are molded in childhood and either reinforced or reshaped throughout life. Use these prompts to write about what you implicitly have expected for your life.
    - In your mind as a child, how did you think life was supposed to be?
    - At your current age, do you still think that way? What do you now expect?
    - But, a change of plans has occurred. Write about that (*But I didn't plan on....*).
    - Are you afraid that you brought this change on yourself? If so, why? How do you think you did this? If not, how did this change occur?
- *Write about some memories—good, bad, and indifferent.* Don't stop to think. List up to 25 or more memories. These memories are like the three stones described in chapter 3 on mourning with our emotions. They give context to life without your loved one by placing it within a broader set of your experiences. Then, choose one memory to write about in detail with a rich tapestry of colors, sizes, shapes, sounds, remembered words,

[13] Some of these journal and poetry exercises are adapted from: Susan Zimmermann, *Writing to Heal the Soul: Transforming Grief and Loss Through Writing* (NY: Three Rivers Press, 2002).

and tastes. If you want to write one day and become stuck, choose one of these memories to write about.

- *Record your dreams as soon as you wake up.* Or, you may teach yourself to wake up after immediately after a dream to record it. Dreams teach us the mysteries of the unconscious mind, which wrestles our ogres for us or responds to our innermost needs.

Finding hope in grief

Occasionally, read your journal writing. Conditional language (for example, "might have been," "if only I had," "should have been," or "could have done") can be a way of living a fantasy life. It expresses regret or reveals unrealistic expectations that can get in the way of healing. Where you see conditional language, what does it say about your expectations for life? What does it say about your mourning? What information does it provide you about integrating this death? Use this information to teach yourself something new about your grief.

Use the following journal activities to move from the passivity of grief to the action of mourning. As we discussed in chapter 1, grief hits, hurts, slams, blasts, and compels us; but it's passive in that we feel grief and can choose to do nothing with it. Mourning, on the other hand, is the activity of expressing grief. Crying, wailing, visiting and/or decorating a grave, going on a crusade, creating a home shrine, and coming to support group meetings are all mourning activities. Mourning leads to healing, while grief—left untouched—may simply cripple us, covering us with the poor camouflage of the carrier shell.

- *Visit a "healing place" where you can experience a sense of the sacred, and use this setting as your place to write.* Such places can be manmade, like a church, temple, public park, college campus, or even a sensuous coffee bar. Or, a healing place can be of the natural world like a canyon, river, ocean, mountain, forest, or garden. Hear water. Touch trees. Sit on moist grass. Write what wells up in your soul, letting the grace of this healing place overwhelm you with its sights and sounds. If you live in a city, nature is as close as the nearest tree that is budding or shedding its leaves—or even a corner of the zoo where the birds flit freely.

- *Share your writing time or place with others, if you want.* However, try to avoid people whose negative energy saps you or places that create chaos in your mind or spirit. You will know that this negative energy is there if you feel more tired, sad, or lethargic in this space with this person or people around. If negativity surrounds you and you can't simply leave, use writing to express what otherwise might eat at your soul. Write until the negativity or grief is gone—if only for the time being. Then, listen for more positive or spiritually wholesome thoughts from yourself or others.

Writing can help us to live again. Find grace in loss by rediscovering life and choosing to honor your beloved loved one through your own well-lived life. Grace may be fleeting one day and lasting the next, but if we're open to it, grace can come to us all despite our losses—and *sometimes because of our losses.*

- *Write about loss and appreciation.* If you haven't yet come to a more peaceful place in your mourning, don't worry. If you set an intention to heal, you will get there even if it takes a while. For this exercise, begin your writing with the words that open most fairy tales: "*Once upon a time, I had....*" Then, continue by responding to the following prompts:
    - What do I appreciate now about my life?
    - How did my loved one's death propel me to this place?
    - What did I appreciate about my loved one? What do I most appreciate about him or her now?

- What makes my heart break? What makes it smile?

- *Write about losses and graces.* Draw a line down the middle of a piece of paper or use the left- and right-side pages of your journal. Label the left side "losses" and the right side "graces." On the left side, list all the losses that you have experienced in your lifetime, or just list all the losses that are related to the death of your loved one. Then, on the right side, list all the graces you can think of regarding your life, or those regarding the person you have loved and lost. At first, the list of graces may be shorter than the losses. Return to this journal entry several times. Over the days or months, the list of graces will grow longer as you continue to mourn. Using your mind to mourn—as well as your emotions, spirituality, body, and social life—will open your heart to the blessings that have come out of your personal losses.
- *Write about the unexpected in your life.* The words "serendipity," "synchronicity," and "coincidence" are all words expressing the concept of *grace.* These words indicate the experience of finding valuable or positive things that we haven't looked for or expected to emerge from grief-based events. For example, by losing both my brother and then my father within 17 months, I became a best friend to my mother—without loss, this grace might have escaped us forever. By losing my sister, I gained a stronger relationship with my nephew and niece. What graces have come to you because of your loss/es?

Poetry

I'm not a poet. Many of us find poetry writing to be a bit frightening. Sometimes we fear poetry writing because we think that we have to find rhymes for each line. The neat thing about poetry writing, however, is that none of us has to worry about other people reading it unless we choose to share it. Our mourning-based poetry won't be graded or judged unless we give it to someone for that purpose.

Poetry does not need rhymes or a particular number of letters, syllables, or words per line unless we choose to follow the established pattern of particular types of poems. The only two things that poetry really needs are carefully selected words that describe and detail our point of view and—usually—punctuation that allows us to make sense of the words. The word choices are the most important because by finding just the right words to express our grief, we work cognitively with that grief in a true mourning activity. In poems, we whittle away the unnecessary words and finely tune the most expressive ones that convey the point.

The following are examples of poems written in honor of a beloved loved one:

Memorializing Through Poetry

Death in the Time of Daffodils by Beverly Peterson©

For Joseph Galano, Sr., born on the island of Ischia, Italy, in 1908, and died at age 96½.

Trees downed by last fall's hurricane
Point west northwest,
Perpetually west northwest
(No foliage yet to shroud that hefty compass).
But leaves will come,
Palling the site of death and decay.
They will come soon, since already
Crocuses give way to daffodils
And birds sing up the sun and hold the moon at bay.
How dare you choose this time to die.
Death in the time of daffodils
Defies all nature.
Better to have passed west northwest
Next fall,
Next winter,
Or the next.
Or if I had my way,
Better you should stay.

Cartoons by Christina Lengyel©

He said it was like a cartoon
like the Roadrunner realizing
he wasn't on the ground and
that sound, a whistle while the world
rushes up to greet you. You were always
a Yosemite Sam man yourself
thinking something about tarnation as you fell.
    If it had been a cartoon,
    the power lines would have held
    your weight and bungeed
    you back skyward, higher
    than you had been, not that
    shock and drop I imagine.
A year and some change
and strangely magnified
a few thousand times its size.
Switch out the field and power lines
for buildings.
    And the part about the cartoon—
    it wasn't like a cartoon
    when bodies were burning and bailing
    out of high windows
    and all those freshman eyes roved
    from TV screen to each other—me—
    to see how our own faces looked.
The resident expert on aerial wreckage
was already busy blacking out that day.
These hysterical moments, Wylie Coyote
wouldn't touch with a ten foot stick
of dynamite.

Incarnate by Christina Lengyel©

You, the spark
but not the fire
lying there feeding

Them—the worms.
A hollow cavern where once
You made liquid despair, where
many times you observed the smiles of
Dogs and children.
Your thick jacket is becoming
compost for future generations
of people like you,
But does it recall all the textures
that you felt? Does it even know
its muddy satin blanket?
I feel no more like air for having
Breathed it.
You, the dream—
What was it? To touch
the face of God.
None here shined quite brightly enough
for the tastes of an aviator.
Angels, better pupils than your apples and
the restless worms you
feed yourself to.
For all the words I've called you,
Icarus is best, and yes,
I find the aspirations
of we stones intoxicatingly foolish.

This Man Who Moved by Bill Rettberg©

This Man who moved
Through our lives too fast,
Leaving holes in our hearts
That forever will last,
Gives pause to reflect on that sad lonely place
Where only a memory can now fill that space.
Winds sweep the fields that he once strode,
As through searching for him to haul one more load,
Yet reality bites and the path, it grows cold,
And the winds frantic quest soon will grow old.

The flag he loved so dear still flies every day,
Raised by loving hands that continue his way.
All who loved him honor his power,
Because honesty and decency filled every hour.
There is so much for all to measure,
His worth to us was beyond mere treasure.
That he cared, he loved, and he lived his life his way
Will comfort all 'til our dying day.
So we mourn, we remember and force a small smile,
With our last ride, we'll reunite in a while,
But that does not comfort the time we now dwell,
He's in a better place, but we're left in hell.
We move on; there's nothing else we can do,
His place in our hearts stays secure and so true.
John will be with us as our beings now mend,
Because he will always be your father,
And he will always be my friend.

As this photographic illustration shows, poetry can be a lasting gift given to the bereaved at a funeral or memorial ceremony or after these occasions.

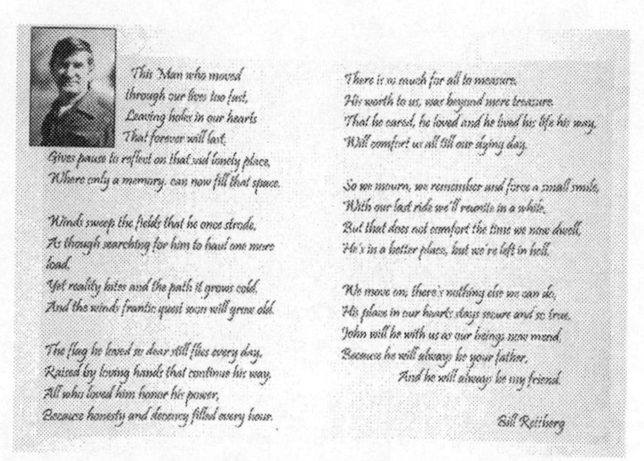

This Man who moved
through our lives too fast,
Leaving holes in our hearts
That forever will last,
Gives pause to reflect on that sad lonely place,
Where only a memory can now fill that space.

Winds sweep the fields that he once strode,
As though searching for him to haul one more load.
Yet reality bites and the path it grows cold,
And the winds frantic quest soon will grow old.

The flag he loved so dear still flies every day,
Raised by loving hands that continue his way,
All who loved him honor his power,
Because honesty and decency filled every hour.

There is so much for all to measure,
His worth to us, was beyond mere treasure.
That he cared, he loved and he lived his life his way,
Will comfort us all till our dying day.

So we mourn, we remember and force a small smile,
With our last ride we'll reunite in a while,
But that does not comfort the time we now dwell,
He's in a better place, but we're left in hell.

We move on; there's nothing else we can do,
His place in our hearts stays secure and so true.
John will be with us as our beings now mend,
Because he will always be your father,
And he will always be my friend.

Bill Reitberg

Poetry as a tribute of love

If you would like to try writing a poem that memorializes your loved one/s, this simple poem structure designed by Susan Zimmermann offers an easy way to express yourself.

Exercise: Writing a Poem

Choose an object that belonged to your loved one and describe it	*List your feelings about the object*
Create similes or metaphors for the object	*Put yourself in place of the object, take on its voice and write from its perspective*

In this example, I wrote about my brother's beloved cowboy boots, displayed on the top of his half-closed casket.

Choose an object that belonged to your loved one and describe it.	*List your feelings about the object*
Tall cowboy boots Dark brown leather Scuffed toes and worn soles Angled heels Useful and used Worn by suburban wanna-be cowboy Wooden boot jack nearby Left atop the closed end of the coffin	Sad, empty boots longing for him Symbols of his liveliness and vivacity Kickers with no place to go Lost, missing their owner Missing him

Create similes or metaphors for the object	*Put yourself in place of the object, take on its voice and write from its perspective*
- Boots like an empty vase waiting to be filled again - Empty boots like an empty home - Filled with his scent, but not with his being - Brown like dusty air, hard to breathe - Worn like an old horse left brooding for a ride	I was crafted by hand from the best cow leather the middle class can buy. My studs and designs were hand wrought to appeal to the rustler in the tamed man, the badass in the gentleman, the Yosemite Sam in the engineer.

After you have written from these prompts, turn the paper over and create your poem. It will practically write itself because you have already done the thinking.

Finally, tweak the poem by checking to see that every word matters and that the punctuation makes the piece more readable to others (if you decide to share it). Everyone in the family can write a poem from these prompts—even the youngest child who may need your help making letters. Children often like to read their poems for the family, which can help them to share difficult feelings. A poetry sharing can lead to healing some of that heavy grief that weighs down the family.

A Non-Poet's Poem

Empty Boots by Beth L. Hewett©

Boots on his coffin, his leathery scent.
Hand crafted, tough hide,
Criss-crossed from rusty barbed wire,
Studded for the tamed rustler.
Scuffed toes and worn heels from years of
the gentleman badass's can-kickin' lope.
Empty boots, empty home.
Our Yosemite Sam, the last pardner gone.

Fiction and Non-Fiction

Of course, writing longer pieces also can soothe the grieving mind and spirit. Depending on how comfortable you are with writing, you may choose to write anything from a short story to a novel, from a short essay to a memoir of life with your beloved. In the play *Wild with Happy*, for example, Colman Domingo uses satire to reflect on his grief about his mother's death.

The following example is a piece of writing that I started exactly nine months to the day after my brother George died. I woke up that morning, unaware of the date, and felt pushed to go right to my computer to write. After I realized the anniversary date, I put the piece away. I returned to it—again somewhat unconsciously—after my father died seventeen months later. Sometimes, when mourning with the mind, the writing writes itself.

Writing Non-Fiction to Work with Grief

Nine Months to Life by Beth L. Hewett©

Death came to me later in life. I was forty-two when my brother suddenly died in a small plane crash. Within one week, I had my first close experience with death, two funerals (one for him and one for his student pilot), and had become the oldest child in a reduced birth family of five. In that week, I found that death is experienced much the same as when we anticipate new life: we count time around life and death in similar ways.

When a woman becomes pregnant, accurate home testing technology allows her to begin by counting the probable number of days since conception. Or, in the absence of knowing the days, she counts the weeks. Someone asks, "How far along are you?" She replies, "Five weeks, sixteen weeks, twenty-one weeks." At some point, the measuring stick of weeks shifts to months plus weeks and she tells her friends, "I'm at eight months now—thirty-six weeks is almost here." If she is overdue, the count restarts at days, moving to weeks if necessary: "Four days overdue." "A week late—when *will* this baby come?"

When the baby finally is born, again the count restarts: first in hours (*"She's ten hours old. Can you believe how tiny her fists are?"*); then in days (*"He's four days old today; I think he smiled at me!"*); then again in weeks (*"Hi, Dad. Yes, she's fine. She's thirteen weeks old, and I think that she'll roll over soon—I can just see how hard she's trying."*). At some point, not quite the same for everyone, we begin to gauge the baby's age in months: *"Oh, yes, he's a real boy all right. He's just four months old, but he's already grabbing for the trucks embroidered on his play mat."* And, for a long time we measure our baby's age in months, from four to six to ten to twelve months and beyond.

In fact, we generally gauge the baby's age in months until about two years old, where the eighteen-month and twenty-three month old infant gives way to the toddler of two and three years, and then to the four- and five year-old preschooler. By then, years have become the way that we measure our lives and we celebrate not the eyelashes that grow in as we feed the infant or the wonders of the first haircut, but the annual milestones of school completed, little league trophies, and graduations, as well as the special events of new jobs, weddings, and home mortgages. Finally, we come full circle to the miracle of grandchildren, who grow from day one and whose lives we track as we have our own child's.

What we don't think about, of course, is the death of our child. We cannot ever consider that possibility until somehow, horribly, it occurs. And then, we restart the count—except that this is the count of death and not of life.

Hours after we learn of the child's death, somewhere the thought grows: *"She was alive just seven hours ago; I know; I kissed her goodbye as she drove off."* In the first days, we stand numb and think silently, *"He's been gone for two days. I should call and tell him that everyone is here, asking, crying, and searching for what to say. He'd appreciate that love."* A bit later, the days turn to weeks and we think, *"Two weeks, dear God, two weeks without her dimpled smile in this world."* And, we count the child's absence in weeks for a long time until, somehow, months go by. Perhaps it is the simple necessity of moving past the weeks to counting time more efficiently that forces the time shift. Or, maybe it is the coming and going of family-shared holidays. In our family, Thanksgiving took us just past the four-month mark from my brother's death; getting through Christmas marked five; and Easter led to nine months. After a year passes, we say, *"I can't believe he's been gone for a year."* But at a year and a half, someone asks and we say, *"She died just eighteen months ago—how can such a short time feel like a lifetime?"*

As time moves forward, we live on and we integrate our loved one's death into our lives. A nephew starts college, a son graduates, and a niece begins driving. All of the adult children move to new houses, new jobs, and new phases of life. Then a friend's child is born and a grandmother blessedly dies, having spent too many years dying to count. Suddenly, when a father dies—shockingly young and only two months after his own mother—it becomes clear that everyone is someone's child and that even contemplating anyone's death is a theoretical activity until it becomes the horrible reality. And the count from gestation to birth to toddler to adulthood to death again is a full circle—necessary to, and inseparable from, a life lived with love for others.

Nine months. In nine months, the typical woman can gestate a baby and give birth to a new life—starting the cycle all over again.

Nine months. On the morning of the nine-month anniversary of his death, my brother visited me in a dream, where for dream-hours I built a small yellow plane to fly in a contest. I never got to fly that plane (named, ridiculously, "Radio Flyer" for the red wagon we shared as children). Instead I spent my dreamtime getting others off the ground, tightening their seat belts, and making sure everyone's fuel tank was full. By the time my own tank was full of the club soda that would make it fly, the race was nearly done and my plane somehow seemed too small to fly, and so I watched the others fly freely in a sky so blue it hurt my eyes.

Almost nine months after George's death, with my father's fatal coronary coming soon to bury him far too early, I realized what my brother was telling me in the dream. *You be the oldest. You watch over the others. But, don't be too slow to fill your plane—life is more than helping others along. Life is flying, too.*

Try writing a piece about grief that you can share through a letter to loved ones, an email, a blog, or other format. Remember that you can keep anything you write completely private as well.

Looking Backward to Mourn

Look at this image of a *sankofa*. A sankofa is a symbol from Ghana that variously means, in the Akan language, "look-back bird" and "*go back and get it.*" This bird reaches behind her, turning her head around to grasp the egg that is on her back. Her feet face forward even while she looks backward. The egg symbolizes that we need to look back and take some things from the past to bring into our future lives. The Ghanaian culture has a proverb that says, "*It is not wrong to go back for that which you have forgotten.*" These people instinctively recognize that sometimes we, as Dr. Wolfelt says, need to go backward in order to move forward.

The Look-back Bird

Sometimes we need to look at our past—go backward—before we can go forward in mourning. Certainly, there are aspects of our past lives and our relationship with the deceased that will help us mourn, heal, and live joyfully again. Looking back means that it is okay, even healthy, to return to the past and contemplate our relationship with the beloved. Rather than dwelling in the past forever, though, the goal is to bring into the future what we can learn from the past, using it to secure a healthy connection with our loved ones, living and deceased. The message of the sankofa is that looking back is a natural, normal, and necessary part of a healthy relationship with the deceased. The act of "going back" to get that relationship is a hopeful one.

We can get help with our grief from a professional grief counselor or another type of helper. If you get stuck or want to explore your grief more cognitively, try working with a skilled grief counselor, coach, or companion. A cognitive therapist, in particular, does what is sometimes called "talk therapy." The process of talking together can lead to new understandings that help to resolve some of the mental-, spiritual-, and heart-based issues of grief.

You may want to seek a grief therapist if:

- You feel stuck—as if you can't make any forward movement in your mourning.
- You realize there are some traumas or family-related habits from your past that may hinder your mourning.
- You have tried a support group and find that to be unhelpful or too uncomfortable for you.
- You have your own sense of how you should be doing with your grief and would like some reassurance or specific help with your progress.

If you decide to work with a grief therapist, coach, or companion, it can be helpful to get a referral from someone you trust—like your grief support group leader, a church nurse, or other health care professional. A licensed therapist is different from an unlicensed, yet possibly certified counselor, coach, or companion. You may expect to pay for any of these services if health insurance does not cover it, but these individuals have different functions.

Any of these helpers should provide you with a sense of safety and respect for your grief and mourning needs.

- **A licensed therapist** will have had special education in psychology and may or may not have had specialized training in grief issues. This individual should be skilled in helping you feel your emotions and providing insight about them.
- **A counselor or coach** may not need a license or certification in your state, but will be a good listener who has experience with or training about grief. Counselors and coaches tend to provide feedback and guidance on next steps that you might take.
- **A companion is someone who is qualified through training and life experience to walk with you on your grief journey**. This person will have experience listening and allowing you to talk about your grief, so that you can teach him or her about your grief. The companion may come from your local church, for example, or may not be affiliated with any particular institution, but he or she should have some grief training.

It's a good idea to decide what you want from a professional who will talk about grief with you. You don't need to work with the first person who comes recommended or whom you meet. When possible, interview several people. Things to ask in an interview include:

- Have you had personal experience with grief? If so, what are some of the ways you have worked with your own grief? (personal background)
- Have you had professional training to help me with my grief? If so, what? (professional background)
- What do you believe about grief, mourning, and healing after a loss like mine? (grief philosophy)
- What other specialties do you have training in? This question enables learning whether this person may be helpful in connecting the grief to other issues that might hinder your healing: for example, alcohol or other substance abuse, childhood trauma, sexual abuse, and physical abuse. It also enables learning whether this person prefers to work with children, teens, adults, and/or families. (client preferences)

- How will we decide how long and how often to meet? (processes for working together)
- What are your charges? Do you take my insurance? (financial considerations)

In sum, talking about your grief in either a group or private setting can be helpful. Chapter 7 describes some of the benefits and processes for choosing a helpful grief support group.

Other Cognitive Mourning Activities

- Do brain work like word-find puzzles, crossword puzzles, and Sudoku to keep your mind active. These are not mourning-based activities *per se*, but they can help with mental clarity and focus when the mind otherwise is wandering into grief that you can't address at that particular time.
- Do relatively mindless handwork like quilting, counted-cross-stitch, needlepoint, or coloring when you want to think about and work with the grief.
- Create a six-word summary of life, grief, or mourning to explain your experience to others and yourself. This mental activity requires boiling down and compressing a major life event, which can help with mental clarity and focus around your grief.
- Write a letter to yourself talking about your personal goals for mourning in six months. Self-address the envelope and stamp it. Give it to a trusted friend to mail to you in six months.
- Return to work, but be as flexible as you can with your hours and tasks. Your mind has many details to address and, while your job can provide you with something to do outside the home, it can be exhausting. If you're in a position of operating heavy equipment or where mistakes can be dangerous, talk with your supervisor first about whether your grief might affect your performance. Your employment is one area where the ripple effects of grief can be especially serious.
- Play games and sports with others, but be aware of possible mental fatigue. If you become tired when playing, it can lead to

hurt feelings, as well as scratches and dents in the new family setting of life without the deceased. Therefore, be careful of what you say and how you say it to others who also are grieving the loss.

What other mourning activities can address or use your mind?

Chapter 7

Mourning Socially

When we grieve, sometimes we just want to be alone. However, I think that most of us don't mean that we want to be totally alone—just temporarily alone with the certain knowledge that other people are ready to join us when we're ready for them.

In a way, when we're grieving, we want what we want when we want it! Grief can be a bit capricious that way.

There is a distinct social realm of mourning just as there are the emotional, spiritual, physical, and cognitive realms. The social realm involves our desires and need to be with other people. As with any other realm in our grief journey, we must find our unique balance.

> *The friend who can be silent with us in a moment of confusion or despair, who can stay with us in an hour of grief and bereavement, who can tolerate not knowing... not healing... not curing... that is a friend indeed.* Henri Nouwen

Grieving in a Group

One way to grieve in the social sphere is in the company of a committed grief support group where the hard work of mourning can occur. Remember that mourning is the work that allows grief to be addressed;

the grief is suffocating if it's only to be felt and not expressed. Grief groups, which take a variety of shapes that usually are determined by their purposes, can help many people.

- *On-going, drop-in group.* This kind of group meets regularly, often year-round, and it welcomes people at any stage of their bereavement. Sharing about the grief is the primary purpose of this group. No registration typically is needed. Therefore, it provides an opportunity for the bereaved to meet as often and as regularly as needed, which differs because our grief is unique. Although there may not be a specific cost, free-will offerings may be accepted.
- *Time-limited, committed member group.* This kind of group requires some kind of a time commitment from the members, usually between six to twelve weeks. It may be restricted to those who have been bereaved for a particular amount of time. Sharing about the grief usually is a part of this work. Generally, it focuses on certain topics or themes, and it may have a component that includes reading a book or particular activities. There may be a cost for resources.
- *Time-limited retreat.* A retreat typically is designed for a limited time, typically a weekend or week. It seeks to provide a relaxing place—often, away from home—for exploring difficult grief issues. Usually, time for sharing about the grief is a part of the retreat schedule. Generally, there is a cost for both the retreat and lodging.
- *One-day workshop.* A workshop in grief often focuses on a particular theme or concern—like grief during the holidays or improving our health when bereaved. Typically, a workshop is differentiated from a seminar in that there are hands-on activities with the belief that doing something helps to make the learning more concrete. There may be time for sharing about the grief, but this usually isn't the primary goal of a workshop. Often, there is a cost associated with the workshop time and resources.
- *Part-day seminar.* A seminar provides a short-term learning opportunity (usually one to three hours) focused on a theme or

issue. There may not be opportunities for sharing, and there may not be hands-on activities given the shorter time period involved. There may be a cost for the speaker or learning resources.

Grief-focused groups of all types offer the opportunity to talk about our grief with people who are experiencing similar issues. These people can provide listening ears that aren't judgmental of what we're feeling or experiencing. Such a group should be a safe place where our needs can be addressed in confidence.

Memorializing loved ones in a social group

As bereaved people, we share the need to tell our stories about the deceased's life, illness, accident, hospitalization, and death, as well as our relationship with the deceased, the ripple effects of his or her death, and the many other realities of the death. Spending time with a grief group is an immensely helpful social mourning activity for many people. However, some people are not as comfortable in a group setting; if you don't care for this kind of group meeting after having tried it, it's perfectly reasonable to choose not to return. Be aware, though, that feelings and needs do change over time so you may want to revisit a grief group at another time.

How do you know when group mourning is good for you?

- You feel a need to talk with other bereaved people about your loved one and related grief.
- You're uncomfortable talking about your grief to people you know.

- You're uncertain whether you want to talk, but you want to know whether other people feel the way you do.
- You've tried to "go it alone," and you feel stuck.
- You generally have been doing all right with mourning, but recently have experienced a sense of being newly bereaved or unable to cope.
- You're ready for a different and powerful way to move forward.

What should you expect from any grief group, retreat, or other grief-based social group?

- *Experience and care:* The facilitator should be experienced and caring. He or she should indicate clearly that you're welcome, explain the group rules to you, and keep the group moving to give everyone time and opportunity to talk.
- *Clear rules:* There should be a clear set of ground rules that make sense in the context of the group. Such ground rules should include:
    - *Confidentiality:* What is said in the room stays there. While participants are free to share their growth with loved ones, no one's names or specific circumstances should be discussed outside the meeting.
    - *No advice giving:* People should have the opportunity to talk without having to fend off unwanted advice. Listeners should be guided to offer their support; however, the group should not devolve into a series of suggestions and off-topic discussions.
    - *Opportunity:* Everyone in the group should have the chance to talk during the course of the meeting. Likewise, if a participant wants to "pass" and not speak on a particular day, that need should be respected by all.
    - *Sense of safety:* A respectful environment will produce a safe place for participants to be real about their grief and attempts to work with it. The general atmosphere should reflect kindness and generosity.

- *Opportunities to mourn:* There ought to be opportunities to work with the grief in different ways (such as talk, listen, think, hear music, take notes, draw, and write letters) that may help to ground the bereaved in helpful mourning practices.

The work of mourning done in a group isn't necessarily better or easier than doing it alone, but it's a gift that enables others to know and love you and experience your love because they need it, too. Although we may feel broken and unable to be repaired, we need understanding and don't need to be "fixed." Indeed, in a group setting, the work that each one of us does is the work of all of us. We teach and reach each other merely by talking together. In some ways, the grief group enables us to take the opportunity to say goodbye when we may not have had enough time to do so in our loved one's lifetime.

Helpful groups provide safe spaces for mourning. Sometimes—as with retreats and workshops—they offer interactive work. Chapter 4 details how to make a grave blanket, for example, as one activity that not only helps to mourn actively around the holidays but also involves the social interactions of talking about the deceased for whom the blanket is intended.

Another group activity that provides ample time to talk and process the loss is one my co-facilitators and I call "cracked pots." This activity offers a hands-on, yet highly symbolic way to process grief as it currently exists, as well as to predict how it will change over time.

1. Plan about two hours for the group's work. If the group is very large and needs to be split, plan for about three to seven people in smaller groups.

2. Purchase or find three to four inexpensive, decorated ceramic flower pots. Each pot should be of a different color or distinctive design.

3. Provide two to three hot glue guns and the same number of black writing markers.

4. Cover a table with paper to protect it.

5. Break all of the pots into some large and some small pieces using a hammer or other tool. Naturally, some pots will have more pieces than others.

6. Using the marker pens, have everyone write some emotions about the death or grief on the inside of various pot pieces.

7. Using hot glue guns (and being very careful not to cut yourself on the pot pieces or to burn yourself on the glue gun), work together to piece the broken pots back together. There is no need to have a glue gun for every person. A rich result of this activity comes from cooperating to share the materials and help each other find the correctly fitting ceramic pieces.

8. After the group has put the pots together as best as possible, take some time to talk about this activity.

   - What was it like to put the pots together? What was the effect of doing this work in a group setting?
   - What do the repaired pots say to you about your grief and mourning? In other words, how do they symbolize your unique grief and mourning?
   - Look at the repaired cracked pots. Which one most looks like your grief right now? How? Why?
   - Do any of the pots illustrate your goals for mourning? If so, which one/s? Why?

Mending broken hearts with cracked pots

Finding Social Outlets

Grief groups have a specific purpose of talking about and working through the grief using group talk and other mourning activities. We can address our grief in other social settings, too. In fact, sometimes it's surprising how much mourning we can do socially. But, it can be hard work to make that mourning happen.

The funeral and memorial ceremonies are designed to provide social connection when we're grieving. Sometimes, the bereaved find that there are many people who are willing and eager to connect with them in the days immediately before and shortly after the funeral. Then, interactions with others taper off as our friends and family return to their daily lives. Around that time, the shock of the death begins to wear off and we become lonelier than we ever thought was possible. *Where did everyone go?*

Most people mean no disrespect or harm when they stop contacting the bereaved as often as they did right after the death. In fact, they may believe that their solicitous calls and questions actually bring more pain because they remind us of the death—as if we had forgotten it happened! We're especially susceptible to hurt feelings at this time (remember the high need to be understood and the low capacity to be understanding?), and we can seriously misunderstand others' actions. And our friends and family, as many of us know, can say incredibly unhelpful things like "*buck up,*" "*this, too, shall pass,*" "*you're very lucky he didn't suffer,*" and "*she's in a better place.*" Such awkward phrases usually are meant well, but simply come off as odd and unsupportive.

Setting an intention to heal and mourning actively give us an opportunity to be generous to the gaffes of our friends and family. It's best not to rely on others to create a social life for us after bereavement, but it's good to include them when possible in our mourning. Here are some ways to involve our friends and family that can work for us as mourners.

Practicing Avoidance

Sometimes, we just don't want to explain to others what's happened to our loved one. Two years after Kathy's death, my brother-in-law was still meeting people who didn't know that she had died. He, like other bereaved people, tends to dread such moments. They rake up pain at unexpected times and no matter how much time has gone by, our throats catch with tears.

When you don't want to be around people you know, it's okay to go where no one knows you're grieving. Crowded places like a concert, museum, or movie theater can give a sense of being with others without actually requiring you to say a word to anyone, if this is a day when you prefer not to talk. Shortly after George died, my sister-in-law found herself not wanting to explain the circumstances of his death to people that she knew in town. She began grocery shopping in a neighboring town where people didn't know her. This action provided her chances to be around others while not interacting on any meaningful way with them. Certainly it's fine to choose our own places of safe avoidance.

Interacting with People We Know

Just as it's okay to go where others don't know us, we can go where people do know us. For example, if you're in more of a mood to interact superficially, you might happen into people you know in the local department store, the gym, the dog park you frequent, or other such places. These people often know that we're grieving and can offer a light connection to the lives we had before the curtain of grief came down.

If we want a deeper connection with people, then we might need to initiate it ourselves. As I explained above, at about the time that the bereaved become really lonely, people often stop calling. That doesn't mean we aren't considered or that our loss has been forgotten, but it can feel that way. This is when taking action is important (and difficult) on our parts. If friends don't call and ask you out, call them and make the date. Assume that they mean well and that they may be shy since you're grieving and they don't know what to say.

Think of it this way: I'm allergic to all fragrances—perfume, cleaning chemicals, air deodorizers, potpourri, fragranced tissue, the whole shebang. I let people I see frequently know about my allergy because it's irresponsible on my part not to. No one can know my needs if I don't make them clear. However, I still may encounter a heavily fragranced house or bathroom or even a strongly perfumed seat partner at church.

The fragrance is very difficult for me to be around, but if I take offense—as if this person has deliberately perfumed herself or the area to make me uncomfortable—not only will I not get my needs met, but I also will make everyone around me uncomfortable.

Similarly, when we grieve, we believe that people may "know" something about our needs. "*Isn't it obvious?*" we think—but they seem oblivious to those needs. If we haven't told people about our grief—explicitly told them—then our needs or expectations can't be met. Even if we've told them, people may go about their typical activities, forgetting the special-need requests that we have made. We should take responsibility, of course, for any unstated needs because it is unfair to expect others to read our minds for the specifics of our grief. When loved ones and friends seem to ignore the special requests or the non-apparent needs of the bereaved, we do well to not take offense. Instead, we should educate them when possible and, if necessary, leave a situation that feels intolerable.

Here are some activities that enable us to interact socially and helpfully to mourning:

- *Go to a church, senior center, or other regular social gathering like your home owner's association, the school parent/teacher association, AARP, Red Hats, or the American Legion.* Get to know new people there, and introduce yourself on your own terms. Become the unofficial greeter who welcomes newcomers, for example. If you are widowed, decide how you want to be called whether by first or Mr./Mrs./Ms. and last name. Regardless of who you've lost, be as open or as closed as you choose. Decide how much of your life and grief you'll choose to reveal. If you meet a fellow bereaved person, treat him or her like you want to be treated *whether or not you reveal your own bereavement.* You're in charge of your choices. Knowing this fact can make healing easier for you.

- *Indulge in a hobby with others.* Learn to make pottery, cook new foods, help at the community college theater, or volunteer at the library. If you have extra time, these kinds of activities can bring a sense of purpose. During these kinds of activities, you don't have to think actively about your grief, which actually allows your mind to work on it subconsciously. Learning new things in a social setting can lead to helpful thoughts after the activity is done.

- *Eat with others.* If you're newly alone, you know that it can be very difficult to cook for one person. If you do cook, it can be difficult to swallow the food, no matter how appetizing. One way to find others to eat with is to invite a friend to lunch. Don't wait for the invitation because it may not come when you want or need it. Another way to eat with others is to become a regular at a local diner or fast food restaurant, where other bereaved and lonely people tend to eat. Meeting others is a good way to become and stay connected, as well as to improve your appetite. My only caveat is that eating fast food regularly can be very bad for your health. Try to maintain a reasonable balance.

- *If you are invited somewhere and your calendar is open, accept the invitation.* One bereaved man that I know has made it a rule to accept all invitations from family and friends because he wants these people to know he appreciates their efforts to include him. However, it's also part of his rule that he does not stay any longer than he truly wants or is comfortable. Staying only as long as you feel you can is a way to honor your intention to heal your unique grief.

- *Whenever you can and need to—by Internet chat, the phone, or over a cup of tea—talk about your loved one with people who care and understand.* There's no rule that you're allowed to grieve only for a few months. You will need to talk about your loved one forever because your job as a mourner is to integrate his or her death into your life—not to shove him or her out of your life! Use your loved one's name around the people you want to socialize with; doing so overtly gives them permission to use this name, too.

In all social settings, we must look for a healthy balance. As often as you can, do something socially nourishing or fun with others. It can be something that you have always enjoyed doing, something new like learning to play challenging games of dominoes, or something educational like teaching others a hobby that your loved one also enjoyed. The way to ensure that your social life includes helpful mourning activities is to plan them in. The way to ensure an ongoing social life is to balance these activities so that you, your family, and your friends do and talk about other things, too.

Letting Animals Soothe Us

Animals provide amazing connections that enable healing on the social level. Let's face it: sometimes we just don't want to be around people! At those times (and others), animals offer themselves in genuine and unconditionally loving ways. Animals reach out to all of us in grief—reading our sorrow accurately—and nudge us to connect with them. Children and adults both can benefit from animals when grieving.

Animals give us the opportunity to fulfill our human needs for touch and hugs when our beloved is gone. Most domesticated animals will allow us to pet, hug, groom, and otherwise handle them. Smaller animals like to curl up and sleep with us. Animals remind us that life goes on because their needs must be addressed every day even when we forget to get enough sleep or food for ourselves. Following the animal's lead, we can be guided back to regular patterns of sleeping, eating, and grooming.

Love puppies

Cats and dogs (as well as horses, rabbits, ferrets, and birds) show a remarkable awareness of the human emotions that surround them. They know when we are approachable both in happiness and sadness, and they know when to stay away. Animals are good barometers of our grief that way.

I like to tell bereaved people about emotional leaking and pets:

- If I'm taking care of my grief in positive ways, I may cry and my dogs will curl up with me, possibly try to lick my face, and may audibly sigh in my arms.
- However, if I'm leaking my emotions—just being grumpy or complaining about something related to my feelings—in other words, if I'm not being honest and open with my feelings, then the dogs tend to look at me warily from the other side of the room. They're not sure of their welcome and prefer to stay out of the way until they're more certain.
- Beyond leaking, of course, there's a potential for emotional explosions that blow up in the animal's face. In that case, instead of just letting the dogs out when they need to go, I might yell at them for being under my feet or for needing my attention when I don't want to give it. Similarly, I might shout at the computer for freezing or needing a reboot. That explosive anger causes my dogs to run away from me—afraid and unsure of our relationship. They know when my emotions make me an unsafe person.

Animals offer us immediate feedback regarding our responses to them. They're unbiased and nonjudgmental. They don't care if I haven't taken my shower or combed my hair. They don't judge based on appearance but on the emotions we experience. They tend to adjust quickly and directly to our relations with them. Talk isn't necessary because they understand nonverbal communication. Their language is one of presence, bonding when it's safe to do so, and consistency. They often will look deeply into our eyes when humans are afraid to connect so deeply. We can thank our animal friends for giving us unconditional love and honest feedback.

Horse therapy

The following are some ways to include animals in our social sphere when mourning:

- *Keep your pet.* Upon being bereaved, if you have a pet, keep it if at all possible. The need to care for the pet (providing water and food, as well as exercise) will help you to stay grounded in the everyday world while managing grief. The pet also may connect you to pleasant memories with your loved one.
- *Get a pet.* Consider getting a pet if you're lonely. However, remember that any pet needs care that you may not be prepared to give while grieving and mourning. Before you commit, try pet sitting for a relative or friend. This pet may not be the one you would choose for yourself, but if you resent the time and care it needs, then getting your own pet is a bad idea for now.
- *Interact with animals.* Visit and volunteer at the local animal shelter or find a 4-H club. You can enjoy the benefits of a loving animal's connection without the additional work of caring for it at home since grieving usually is a challenging time when change is difficult.
- *Walk a dog.* That always attracts people who want to admire and chat with you about the animal. Throw a ball at the dog park and watch all the dogs run—some will run as far from the ball as they can get! Watching my dogs tumble over themselves to get the ball first makes me laugh. I try to watch them play twice

a day to make sure that I'm getting pleasant interaction with them.

- *Consider animal assisted therapy.* This kind of interaction can be found through your therapist, local phone directory, and the Internet. Equine, or horse, therapy is an interesting area. Horses, which are prey animals (unlike cats and dogs), are especially aware of human emotions and how those emotions can affect them directly. With an equine specialist and a psychotherapist, people can learn a great deal about how to mourn or how to unblock grief by interacting with these large animals. Some programs even use the horse as a canvas for the bereaved to paint their grief. Programs for both children and adults are available.[14]

Using Humor to Mourn with Others

I can find humor in my life just by watching myself go through daily motions. Putting my warmed-up lunch into the refrigerator instead of on a plate amuses me (when it does not annoy me!). Throwing away my dirty clothes instead of putting them into the laundry bin can make me smile. Walking into the empty house announcing loudly that I have parked my car on the roof instead of the garage evokes laughter—or, at least, a shaking of my head. There's ironic humor in the act of talking to our deceased loved ones while driving—we can be thankful that law requires everyone to have a hands-free device for cell phoning so that people don't think we're just crazy drivers talking to ourselves.

In truth, I'm not alone with those moments. I'm in close mental contact with an image of my husband or mother or someone else. The moments are funny in the context of knowing what others would think of my goofs. These humorous moments are all the more ludicrous because invisible others would find them silly. Laughing in an empty movie theater rings hollow while laughing with others in a full theater shares the amusement. Humor certainly works when we're alone, but it's funnier when shared,

[14] Check the Internet for programs like Chesapeake Therapeutic Riding (http://www.chesapeaketherapeuticriding.org/) and Spring Reins of Life (http://www.springreinsoflife.org/)

which is why, of course, we share our goofs with others—we want them to laugh with us in reality and not just in our minds.

It's important to share humor when grieving. When we tell funny stories of the deceased at the funeral, for example, it isn't to make fun of him or her. We tell these stories and laugh together to find the common connection that the humorous situation engenders. Grief can be so desperately sad and painful that sometimes only humor can lift us out of that terrible place. I advise you to find kind humor in any situation you can.

Whenever possible, mourning with others can involve shared humor. That might just be watching the same television show to discuss later. Or, it may be watching the show by yourself but with the beloved deceased in mind—what she or he would think about the humor is something that you will always share together.

When grieving, I often choose a particular situation comedy that I otherwise don't watch (for example, "The Simpsons" or "Everybody Loves Raymond") and watch as many episodes as I can—just to have the chance to laugh. I turn on the comedy channel to catch jokes, skits, and sketches that are irreverent and make fun of everything. Recently, I have found a 24-hour comedy radio station that makes me smile and laugh while I drive.

Laughter is a critical key to my health when I'm mourning. One of my favorite words in the world screams laughter to me. It is the German word *Backpfeifengesicht*. Try to say it. This odd-sounding word literally means "face that cries out for a fist in it." While I don't recommend punching anyone in the face, it amuses me to think about the real-world need this word fills. Think of this wonderful word when someone speaks nonsense and urges you to "get over" your grief or suggests that "there are many fish in the sea"! It can help you to smile and shrug off that particular hurt.

Jokes are told among people. Some are shared verbally, but these days, many are shared through email or social media like Facebook. People—our social groups—are what make jokes so funny.

Some jokes remind us of the brevity of life and can help us to put death into a different perspective:

Grief Humor

Two 90-year-old women, Rose and Barb had been friends all of their lives. When it was clear that Rose was dying, Barb visited her every day. One day Barb said:

"Rose, we both loved playing women's softball all our lives, and we played all through High School. Please do me one favor: when you get to Heaven, somehow you must let me know if there's women's softball there."

Rose looked up at Barb from her deathbed and said: "Barb, you've been my best friend for many years. If it's at all possible, I'll do this favor for you." Shortly after that, Rose passed on.

A few nights later, Barb was awakened from a sound sleep by a blinding flash of white light and a voice calling out to her, "Barb, Barb."

"Who is it?" asked Barb, sitting up suddenly. "Who is it?"

"Barb—it's me, Rose."

"You're not Rose. Rose just died."

"I'm telling you, it's me, Rose," insisted the voice.

"Rose! Where are you?"

"In Heaven," replied Rose. "I have some really good news and a little bad news."

"Tell me the good news first," said Barb.

"The good news," Rose said, "is that there's softball in Heaven. Better yet all of our old buddies who died before us are here, too. Better than that, we're all young again. Better still, it's always springtime, and it never rains or snows. And best of all, we can play softball all we want, and we never get tired."

"That's fantastic," said Barb. "It's beyond my wildest dreams! So what's the bad news?"

"You're pitching Tuesday."

Some will say that life is uncertain. It certainly is. Life is short, too. Eat desert first whenever you can! Laugh whenever possible!

What other mourning activities can address your social needs?

Part 3

Preparing for Grief in Our Lives

Grief will happen in our lives. It's unavoidable. If we love, we will lose someone who's beloved. If we lose that person or people, we'll grieve. There's no sense in trying to avoid grief because the only results of avoidance will be loneliness and frustration—and unresolved grief waiting in the wings. Grief and sorrow are gifts that make us fully human and provide both perspective and opportunities for love.

This section of the book offers ways to engage with an impending death—whether our own or that of another loved one. It's not intended to be comprehensive of all the issues that arise around an upcoming death.

We can comfort our loved ones before they die with various actions. Being generous with our dying loved ones can go a long way toward both easing them as they die and easing our own grief. Similarly, we can connect with our loved ones in positive ways before we are dying or dead. In some ways, we can make their grief easier to bear because of our own generosity of spirit.

Chapter 8

Pre-Mourning Activities

Because death comes to all of us, we must learn to be open to its potential.

In chapters 1 and 2, I said that our contemporary American culture doesn't handle death very well. Culturally, we implicitly learn that death is optional. We seem to think someone else will die—or, we think that they cannot die. As children, we like to think that our parents will die first, but sometimes that doesn't happen. As parents, we believe that it's the right order of the world for us to die before our children, but that, too, isn't a certainty. Or, as spouses, we want to think that we'll die before the spouse—so that we'll not be the ones suffering the grief and years without the beloved. We think our spouses are so much stronger than us and would handle our loss better. That isn't true either.

Life and death just don't work the way we think they should or the way we want them to.

As bereaved people, we know the pain of grief. Because we do, we can do some things to ease our loved ones into death—things that also will help us and our families grieve well by mourning actively. Additionally, we can do some things that can help our loved ones to mourn healthfully before we die and after.

Helping Our Loved Ones to Die

When George was killed in the plane crash and my father died from a heart attack, there was nothing to do except grieve. However, when Kathy was actively dying, there was time left to do some of the initial work of mourning. She was taken to a hospital ten days before her death. There, she received medications and fluids that relieved some of the cognitive disorder she was suffering and revived her spirit and appetite for a few days. Two days later, in agreement with her written wishes and given her terminal condition, medicine was withdrawn. We huddled in a holding pattern as we waited for her to die. Family and friends found it difficult to be with her in any natural way—often, our conversation was stilted and awkward.

It was difficult to believe that my sister actually would die. But the hospital's doctors and nurses assured us it was so. And the insurance company seemed to agree, ordering that she be moved to a nursing home facility for hospice care. And, after three days without medications, she stopped eating, became less lucid, and started to sleep more and more. It seemed that death would come whether we were ready or not.

We did not talk about how we would breathe and think and live after Kathy died.

In her illness and emotional torment, she previously had cut off contact with most of the family. She expressed that it would make it easier for us to forget her when she died. She was wrong. Despite attempts to reconnect, it was impossible to do so. Her husband and children took the brunt of her illness and coped as best they could with an awful situation.

I took those dying days as opportunity to be with Kathy as much as I was able. I wasn't able to do that every day; some days, I just had to take a break from the sadness of the situation, and other life tasks had to be accomplished. However, despite mixed emotions—including my own anger and grief—I will never be sorry that I spent the days I did with her. It was my chance to brush the hair from her eyes, wash her face, wipe some tears, stroke her cheek, and touch her body with my deepest love. I gave her a manicure, massaged her hands and feet with rich moisturizer, and sang her some songs. I told her again and again that she was, indeed, incredibly loveable. And, I wracked my brain trying to sort out how this train wreck had happened.

> *The family exists for many reasons, but its most basic function may be to draw together after a member dies.* Stephen King

One of Kathy's legacies to me is what I learned about death, dying, and about preparing for mourning before death has come. My sister opened her heart to us, bared her soul, and gave us the opportunity to confront some of our grief even while she lay dying. I experienced something of what the phrase "passed away" means. Of course, Kathy's death was as unique as our family's grief, and what we experienced won't fit everyone's situation. Nonetheless, here are a few things I learned that may assist you:

- *Talk to the medical professionals about what is happening.* While all of us were curious as to the dying process, the best information we received came from the hospice nurses—not the doctors. They both talked to us about what dying looks like. For example, they explained that dying people sometimes rally near the end, which can cause the family to believe that the condition has improved. Knowing this can help to guard against the shock of an inevitable death.
- *Read provided information about the processes of dying and death if you are able.* The hospice nurses provided us with a helpful booklet about how the body begins to shut down and the spirit starts to let go of this world. Without that guide, I don't think I could have believed that death actually would come. It was a stretch for me even with that information. However, with that guide, my family was able to talk together about what we were observing as Kathy lay dying. We had the vocabulary for naming what we were seeing.
- *If he or she can bear it, touch your loved one often.* Some patients have conditions that make it too painful to touch them—as with bone cancer, for example, or a skin-based disease. If touch is possible, however, touching can be incredibly important. Stroke her cheek. Comb his hair or shave his face. Massage her tired hands. Smooth lotion onto dry skin. As people die, their bodies

begin to pool all moisture and hydration into the essential organs and away from less crucial fingers, toes, and limbs. But people still can sense a gentle touch from a caregiver. And you, too, may need that tactile memory of your loved one; you need to remember that you loved him or her all you could.

- *Talk with your loved one.* Tell your loved one that you love her; tell him three, four, five, even ten times. "*I love you*" are words that cannot be said often enough. Tell your loved one all the good things that she or he needs to hear from you—make it real and fierce and tender. Then, when the time is right, let your loved one know that she can go whenever she is ready. Selfishly, I asked my mother to ask Kathy to wait until I got to the nursing home to say goodbye. Wisely, Kathy did not wait. My need to be there didn't supersede her need to leave.
- *Just be with your loved one in silence.* A good friend has taught me that sometimes my own need to do something (anything) overrides what my loved one needs or wants. The antithesis of the advice to talk with our loved ones is to sit in silence with them. Sometimes all they need is our company. Giving our full presence—being there in-the-moment—can be exhausting and challenging. It takes energy to be present to anyone and more so if they are dying. Nonetheless, even our silent presence can be the gift our loved ones most need as they die.
- *Give other people time with your loved one.* I learned that it's very different to say goodbye to a dying person than it is to say goodbye to the deceased. Call people who may care to visit if it's alright with your loved one. It can be healing to provide people who knew or cared about your loved one in different stages of his or her life with the opportunity to say goodbye. What they do with that chance is up to them, but what you will have done is to enable relationships to complete a full circle.
- *Help your loved one with five tasks of dying.*[15] Helping your dying loved one to say these things can be a wonderful gift for him or her and an even bigger gift to those to whom these things are said. You can model for your loved one by taking care of

[15] Angela Morrow, RN. (May 20, 2010). "The Five Tasks of Dying." About.com. http://dying.about.com/od/thedyingprocess/a/5_tasks_dying.htm

these tasks for your own part of the relationship. These tasks are:

- *Ask for forgiveness.* Don't burden anyone's soul with now insignificant facts, but do ask for release from the guilt you may feel from hurting them. We might help the dying person by asking first for forgiveness of our faults and errors. Help your loved one say "*forgive me.*"
- *Offer forgiveness.* Forgive your loved one. Forgive him or her everything that needs to be forgiven—even if you're still angry. Let go of hurtful words and memories. They will not help your loved one die any better nor will they give you any peace in your grief. Help your loved one say "*I forgive you.*"
- *Offer heartfelt thanks.* Giving appreciation to others acknowledges our interconnectedness and the fact that we do not live in a vacuum. Help your loved one say "*thank you.*"
- *Offer sentiments of love.* Saying *"I love you"* is not an easy task for many people. Some people cannot voice those words—even at the end of life—but may be able to write or dictate a letter that provides that message. We're products of our lives, yet love is who we are in essence. Help your loved one say "*I love you.*"
- *Say goodbye.* Sometimes dying people hold onto life in order to see or hear particular loved ones. The need to say goodbye is a powerful one. In some ways, I think, that the saying of goodbye encompasses the other four tasks; yet, they are important in and of themselves. Be there for your loved one; try to get others to their side; use the phone or computer if physical presence is completely impossible. Help your loved one say "*goodbye.*"

- *If you can, surround your loved one with a peaceful environment.* Music, for example, is a place from which we transform. It helps to create conditions for both the dying individual and the grieving loved ones to feel grounded and present in these final days and moments. The musical sounds, colors, artwork, and smells that he or she most would appreciate also will touch your senses as you begin to let your loved one go. For some people, reading scripture, familiar prayers, and poetry can be helpful. Often, a dying person may respond or try to participate in the "Lord's Prayer" even if they have been non-responsive previously.

- *If your loved one wants or needs it, bring in a beautician to wash and style the hair.* People who are dying may not remain aware of how they look. They're doing important work—the work of dying—and their focus is on that crucial job. But we bereaved are looking for kind things to do for our loved ones. If it won't hurt him or her in any way and if it might make the final visits easier, some grooming may be helpful.
- *If you can, begin your active mourning before you have lost your loved one.* Set the necessary intention to heal before the pain becomes any worse. Musician Dan Fogelberg's "The Leader of the Band"—a tribute written to his father who died the next year—strikes me as a beautiful example of intentionally opening oneself to a future death. You won't heal right now and the grief will come with your loved one's death, but intention makes healing possible in your future. Talk with others in the family and relationship circle about the ways you'll mourn together. Talk about your beloved's life. Promise to say his or her name often. Express to each other what it means to be together at this difficult time. Most of all, be kind to one another. This is a good time to forgive each other any grudges and to share your essential loving spirit with one another. Your peacemaking will change the atmosphere in the dying individual's room to enable everyone to feel the peace.

I have learned that a peaceful death can be a deeply spiritual and beautiful experience for the family. While they still will grieve, they often find great comfort in having been present for such a death.

Helping Our Loved Ones with Our Eventual Deaths

When I die, people will miss me. For example, my husband, son, and daughter-in-law, and my mother and brother—if I predecease any of them—will have to adjust to life without me. I'll leave behind a few dear friends, people I have known long, and those I have just met. This isn't my ego speaking; it's reality.

When you die, you also will leave grieving people behind. That is a fact. It's no use telling them not to grieve because they will anyway, and they may feel guilty about not meeting your (unrealistic) expectations.

If this book has taught us anything, it has taught that grief shared and mourned actively is grief diminished by healing. We can help our loved ones in their grief before we even die by thoughtfully and consciously leaving them a legacy of our lives with them.

A major key to grieving well is to learn about grief and active mourning. To that end, share this book and what you have learned from it with your loved ones when they next experience grief. Don't wait until your impending death.

What we don't know frightens us the most. When I was twenty-six, I got ready to give birth to my son. We lived in Germany, where my husband served in the U.S. Army. My mother couldn't be there for the birth and I didn't have close friends around me. Consequently, when fellow Army wives talked about childbirth pains, I became quite frightened of the impending birth. There was a baby the size of a basketball or two in my abdomen, and I knew the prescribed exit for that baby was much smaller than the ball. My labor and delivery were complicated by a few factors, and it was long and painful. But it also was familiar. I learned that labor was like having severe menstrual cramps. Well, I had those every month. If anyone would have given me even a hint that labor was connected to menstrual cramps, I wouldn't have been so scared. Losing that fear would have allowed me to relax a little and be more prepared for the other realities of the labor.

It's the same with grief and mourning. If we can give our loved ones some small hint of what it might feel like to lose us, then they can begin to understand before our deaths that it's possible—hard, but possible—to integrate our loss into their lives.

> *Lost love is still love, Eddie. It just takes a different form, that's all. You can't hold their hand... You can't tousle their hair... But when those senses weaken another one comes to life... Memory... Memory becomes your partner. You hold it... you dance with it... Life has to end, Eddie... Love doesn't.* Mitch Albom

Here are some legacy activities that you can adapt to help your loved ones begin to conceive of your death in healthy ways. The first and the last are, I think, the most important.

- *Practice the first four tasks of dying frequently.* Model how to die by modeling how to live well.
  - Grant forgiveness.
  - Ask for forgiveness.
  - Thank your loved ones.
  - Tell them often that you love them.
- *Do not ask family members to have a celebratory party instead of a funeral.* These requests can make our loved ones feel guilty that they need and want the traditional healing rites of funerals and other ceremonies. Funerals are necessary rites of passage that the living need to accept the initial reality of death. Instead, ask your family members to tell you what you meant to them in their lives. Give them a chance to talk with you about your relationships. You might open this discussion by first telling them what they mean to you and how their lives have enriched your own.
- *Do not write your own eulogy.* Writing a eulogy is a healing activity for your family and friends to do. If you want something particular in a eulogy, you might share that or provide a book on writing a eulogy like *Good Words: Memorializing Through a Eulogy*, but leave the task of writing it to the living. On the other hand, if you want to write out items for your obituary, which is different from a eulogy in purpose, that may help your loved ones as they newly grieve and need to share the news of your death.

- *Write a will in which you leave certain virtues and values with your loved ones.* Share your generosity with the child who seems most afraid of losing things and your faith with your cousin who is in need of it. Offer your courage to the smallest one in the family and your peacefulness to the family that is most challenged economically. Share in the will why you go to church and what you would love for your family to get from church or similar activities. Tell them what their love has meant to you. Paint a verbal picture of your best memories with each person for whom the will is written. Give them your love of life by bequeathing them your recipes (just what is a pinch of cinnamon or a dash of saffron or a forkful of sour cream?) or other daily life items.
- *Share precious memories in unique ways.* Take the jewelry that you no longer wear but once cherished and give it a new purpose. While that jewelry might have lived for years in a box, you have precious memories attached to it. Create a legacy by making something new of your jewelry, and share it with your loved ones now by telling them the stories attached to it. I had my jewelry made into drum jewelry, and I told my son when and where I got each piece and why it is special to me. When I die, I hope that the drum and its jewelry pieces will

Making a legacy of jewelry

Legacy jewelry on the African drum

remind Russ of a part of me he otherwise wouldn't know. And, he will be relieved of the task of opening my jewelry box and saying to himself, "*Now, what am I supposed to do with all this stuff?*" Similarly, you can repurpose your jewelry by handing down an engagement ring or recasting wedding rings to give to a loved one to cherish.

- *Give loved ones tasks to complete.* Such tasks should be conceived to engender deeper and continued healthy connection with you and with themselves as your loved ones. For example, if you wanted to explore Paris with them and know you won't get the chance to do it, leave them a letter about what you specifically wanted to show them and why. If you can, leave them money earmarked for the trip. If you can't, take a virtual tour with them by leaving the letter in a Paris tour book that will let them explore your favorite places. Better yet, do this with them before you die and tell them it's part of your legacy to them. Other tasks might be to ride in a hot air balloon, learn how to plant and care for a rose bush, or to take a yearly vacation in a series of favorite family spots.
- *Give your most precious goods to loved ones before you die.* Go around your house and select the items that you love or enjoy the most. Consider who might enjoy it when you have died. In the presence of others *and* in writing, leave those beloved items to specific loved ones. Tell them why you are bequeathing the specific object to them. Then, either give the item to them now, while you are living, or thank them for allowing you to continue to use it until you die. Casting off our attachment to our things brings everyone potentially greater peace around inheritance issues. As a bonus, it fosters our ability to let go of the things of this world.
- *Write letters or stories about yourself.* It isn't too late to share stories of our childhoods or marriages—the kinds of things that indicate how we became the people that we are. Our loved ones will want to know about us in ever more deep ways when they mourn our passing. Tell them now or write them out for sharing later. When you share something deep of yourself, others can treasure it. However, I believe that dark

or painful secrets—*if they need to be revealed at all*—should be shared before you die so that your loved ones and you can work together through any pain that opening such secrets may cause.

- *Use photographs to share your life.* Have a memory bracelet made of your family, like the one I gave my mother. Then, tell your family how you want it shared when you die—or, better still, have one made for each interested family member. Ask them what they might like or surprise them with a memento of you and the family. Or, make a memory book for each child and grandchild from the hundreds of photographs collected over the years. Scrapbook with the photos or have them made into a video or YouTube montage. Include photos of yourself, so they can enjoy memories of you, too.
- *Start a new tradition now.* An example is one that I learned from a fellow grief companion whose father bought an oversized Christmas card for his wife and signed it each year of their marriage with a different love saying and date. His widow now cherishes that card above items with more monetary value. His daughter began doing the same as a way of marking Mother's Day for her mother. Such traditions carry both love and story, teaching new generations the history of their family's connections.
- *Make something with your loved ones that represents your relationships.* If there are children or grandchildren, make something with them that they can cherish. For example, use plaster of Paris to make handprint impressions that show how you are connected; intertwine index or pinkie fingers, for instance. Do something like this regularly because it's likely you'll live a long and healthy life.
- *Give the gift of literacy through your voice.* Record yourself reading a book to future grandchildren who haven't yet arrived. Current technology enables us to do this within certain children's books—and to individualize those books with the child's name. But it also is possible to use a digital or video recorder and to place the files on the computer or Internet to read lengthier books for the children. I loved reading

C. S. Lewis' *Chronicles of Narnia* series with my son, for example. It would be nice to have those books recorded for my grandchildren or grandnieces and nephews. Best of all, I would get to enjoy them again during the recording.

- *Most importantly, practice forgiveness and be the essence of love.* Forgive everyone that needs your forgiveness, and do it in their presence if humanly possible. Try not to die with grudges on your heart because your loved ones will struggle with these grudges in their grief. There are mourning activities to help when dealing with forgiveness, but no activity is better than the real thing. Similarly, ask forgiveness of whomever you should before you die. Forgiveness from others will lighten your spirit, but it also will lighten theirs—enabling them to mourn your death more cleanly. To whatever degree possible, express tender feelings for everyone you love while you are still alive. Say "*I love you*" as often as you can to each person who needs to hear it. Accept it when they say they love you. If possible, hug, touch, and caress your loved ones as a tactile way to show your feelings for them.

Pre-planning a Funeral

Another way to pre-mourn is to pre-plan with our families what we would like by way of funeral and memorial services. It can be helpful to talk together about how we want to be treated after death because ritual and ceremony are especially important when people are newly bereaved and without words for the grief.

As I said earlier in chapters 2 and 3, I don't recommend an immediate "celebration of life" that by its nature prohibits family members from feeling as if they are allowed to cry in their grief. It's important for the dying to recognize that grief and mourning are natural, normal, and necessary and that trying to eliminate pain about death in favor of celebrating a life invalidates a loved one's grief. It really isn't possible to spare loved ones their pain, and it isn't helpful to dictate happiness when sadness is most common and appropriate.

Therefore, in preparing your own family for your ultimate death, it's healthy to discuss rituals and ceremonies that can help people share their grief with family and friends. Decisions include whether a funeral parlor, public space, or home setting would be best for a ceremony. It's also helpful to consider whether you would want a particular type of casket and burial (when and where) or cremation (with cremated remains to be buried, interred in a columbarium, kept in the home, or scattered in a ceremonial way). While taking an active role in any part of the body preparation and funeral doesn't eliminate grief and the need to mourn, these actions are one-time only opportunities for people to connect physically to their deceased loved one; as such, these activities can be remarkably healing.

The "Traditional" Funeral

Professional undertakers and funeral homes emerged in America during the mid-nineteenth century when the practice of sending Civil War soldiers' bodies to their families necessitated embalming them. Funeral homes gained even more popularity in the twentieth century, possibly because Americans became more mobile and began moving away from their ancestral and birth towns in high numbers. Increasingly often during those years, funeral homes—designed to look like formal in-home parlors—offered a "home-like" atmosphere for accommodating large gatherings that families may not have been able to host in their own houses, and people began to rely on funeral professionals for after-death care.

Funeral professionals care for the deceased's body by preserving and preparing it for public viewing. Embalming is a way of preserving the body until everyone can gather for a funeral, which may take a week or more. It involves surgically draining the body of fluids and replacing them with a preservative that plumps the body and gives it a more life-like presentation than a naturally decomposing body will have. It has become a standard practice to embalm, cosmetically make-up the deceased's face and hands, style the hair, and dress the body in clothes specially chosen by the family.

Funerals differ across cultures and faith bases. *Good Words: Memorializing Through a Eulogy* briefly discusses some common funeral types—religious and otherwise—that include a eulogy of some kind. A good funeral director can help families to decide what kind of ritual and ceremony they want in their funeral, which can include not only a carefully preserved body, but also a wake (or viewing), service (in the funeral home itself or in a church), and cremation and/or burial. Some people mistakenly think that all funerals are religious and opt not to have one for that reason. Choosing to skip a viewing (when the body's condition makes it possible) and funeral ceremony can be a sadly missed opportunity to experience grief in a healing social setting. Skilled funeral directors can help the family to design ceremonies and rituals that suit one's family beliefs and needs.

The Home Funeral

Some people decide to have a home funeral where they manage many of the activities that funeral homes typically do. It can be comforting to have the loved one's body at one's home for bathing, dressing, casketing, viewing, and even for burying. When the loved one is personally washed, dressed, and laid out in bed with familiar things around him or her, mourners can begin to accept the reality of the death in the context of the person's home and life. Contextualizing the loss in one's home aids early grief regardless of the deceased's age—from newly born infant to elderly adult.

The "nontraditional" home funeral setting actually is an old tradition that was lost when funeral homes became more popular in the early twentieth century. The trend toward funeral homes remains today, but it's changing to some degree. While some states require that funeral professionals play a part in the after-death care of a loved one, most allow the kinds of at-home care giving outlined above. Home funerals enable families to personalize the funeral and generally to contain costs by foregoing embalming, professional beautification of the deceased, and pressure to buy expensive caskets. Sometimes people are buried "green" in cardboard caskets decorated by family members or in homemade wood caskets. How, when, and where such burials may occur varies state by state, but the family's grief can be affected positively when they sit with death by caring for their loved-one's body.

It's important to note that not embalming the body quickly reveals hollows in the cheeks and sunken eyes as well as skin blemishes, yet a non-embalmed body can be viewed for several days after death in most circumstances. People who have suffered more violent or traumatic deaths may not be good candidates for this approach. Nonetheless, there can be a simple beauty to the natural dead body when one views death as an expected step in the life journey. Indeed, merely choosing to wash the deceased personally—at home, in the hospital, or in the nursing home—offers a chance to care for, hold, and say goodbye to our loved ones in precious, personalized ways.

Memorial Services

Memorial services most often occur when a traditional or home funeral isn't possible, the funeral included only immediate family members, or the state of the deceased's body necessitated cremation. People can have both a funeral and a memorial service, which can be healing given that rituals can be enacted many times for any one person's death. Memorial services can occur shortly after one's death, years later, or at the marking of a special event such as an anniversary or placement of a gravestone.

The body isn't available for viewing for a memorial service because it already has been buried, cremated, or donated for scientific study. However, families and friends usually display photographs and linking objects (such as work tools, sports equipment, and personal items like books or household things) to represent the deceased loved one. Such services may be religious or have spiritual components, but they don't have to. People often eulogize the deceased, sometimes formally and other times informally as described in *Good Words: Memorializing Through a Eulogy*. Typically, food and informal celebration follow the ceremony as another way of allowing the gathered people to talk with and comfort the bereaved family and each other.

Making the Decision

Sometimes the decision of whether to have a professionally hosted funeral, home funeral, or memorial service is taken from us at the time of death—as is the decision of whether to be buried in sacred ground, interred on the family property, or cremated. Yet when we can help our families with these difficult decisions by discussing our thoughts and preferences, we encourage them to face our eventual deaths *and their own deaths* in potentially healing ways. Pre-planning can make a significant difference for us as we prepare to die and for the newly bereaved, who certainly will appreciate knowing our desires.

What other pre-mourning, legacy activities can help you and your loved ones?

Afterword

How Am I Doing?

Grief and mourning are processes that will continue throughout our lives. In these ways, our relationships with our loved ones also continue. How do we know when the hard work of mourning is bearing fruit? When have we integrated this death into our lives? One way is to see how the six needs of mourning that have guided this book have changed our lives.

The Six Needs of Mourning

1. Accept the reality of the death.
2. Let yourself feel the pain of the loss.
3. Remember the person who died.
4. Develop a new self-identity.
5. Search for new meaning.
6. Let others help you—now and always.

We know that we are accepting the reality of the death when:

- We realize that our loved one has died—and isn't coming back. The boots may still be sitting by the back door, but we know they won't be used. The old toothbrush has been removed from the bathroom, but this change doesn't weigh heavily on the soul.

- We speak about the deceased as dead but know that our relationship with this person continues to live in our hearts.
- We feel hope and positive energy in our lives.

We know that we are allowing ourselves to feel the pain of the loss when:

- We're able to focus cognitively and our interest in life has returned. Watching a movie or reading a book is possible and usually pleasurable again.
- There are light moments in life, and the prospects of "funny" and laughter no longer seem like a betrayal of love.
- We begin to conceive of new traditions that include and recall our deceased loved ones. Some of the previous joy of the holidays is returning, and decorating or gathering with family or friends is no longer so painful that we avoid them.

We know that we are developing a habit of remembering the person who died when:

- We can tolerate—and even find satisfaction in—looking at old photographs and talking about the good and hard times with others who knew the deceased.
- We can listen to a variety of music, including our loved one's favorites, with pleasure and less pain. Sometimes, we may cry, but more often we think fondly of our memories with the beloved.
- We have a solid sense that our relationship with our loved ones has not died with the person.

We know that we are developing a new self-identity when:

- We experience a new confidence in who we are or what we are doing. We have developed work, hobby, or relationship activities that "fit" and feel right in our new lives.

- We are less depressed and less often sad overall. Our most affected physical functions are no longer trapped by the grief. Therefore, we're meeting our physical needs for food, sleep, and exercise with more normal patterns.
- We can choose whether and when we want to talk about our loved ones without guilt, excess pain, or extreme sadness.

We know that we are searching for new meaning when:

- We're comfortable in a chosen spiritual life. Our choice of worship service makes sense to us and provides spiritual benefits. There is less pain in attending services.
- We have a sense of what we would like to do with our lives at this point. The sense may be of a temporary goal or a long-term goal, but it's satisfying to put energy into that purpose.
- We're engaging in activities that are meaningful and fulfilling at deep inner levels.

We know that we are letting others help us when:

- We use alone time for solace and pleasure. Being alone is no longer a way of hiding from the world. Our private thoughts are welcome and can bring comfort and pleasure.
- We can tolerate being around other bereaved people and feel compassion toward their pain because we know the support we have received has helped us. Their pain does not always trigger our own sadness.
- We're finding new relationships—not as a replacement for the deceased but as an addition to our current lives.

Think about your own grief journey. In what other ways do you experience healing and hope in your life from doing the hard work of mourning?

> *The soul would have no rainbow if the eyes had no tears.*
> Minquass Native American Proverb

Where Will This Journey Take Me?

Grief comes on us like a curtain—like the before and after of any significant emotional event and we reside for a while in the liminal space of "in between." There always will be a sense of the before and the after and there will always be some grief. But, it's necessary to recognize that curtain consciously and journey willingly with the grief in order to integrate our losses. Doing so enables us *to continue living* while we are still alive and breathing.

Grief honors the human condition, and it gives us a way to ponder the immensity, generosity, and power of love. We ask ourselves: "*What's my purpose in still living when my beloved (spouse, child, parent, sibling, or friend) is gone?*" Coming to an enlightened sense of this purpose requires the hard work of mourning through talking to others, reading, writing, enacting grief, and simply continuing to live.

The work of grief isn't easy or pleasant, but it's the *going through it* that enables us to incorporate loss into our lives. My grief for any one person is not time-limited as much as it is something that I must embrace and pull into myself. No one else knows my answers. You'll come to answers for yourself, as I must do for me. I believe that I'm a better person for having lost close loved ones because I have become more fully human in my journey through their loss. Emotionally, I'm more alive and aware of the brevity of life, so I appreciate it more. I'm therefore grateful to my grief.

We both love and miss our loved ones. Getting better—integrating the loss into our current lives because we are still alive—is not an act that betrays the deceased loved one but an act that embraces our own lives. Guilt is unnecessary. Our healing is what our loved ones want for us.

It's an odd fact that the closer a ship draws to a lighthouse, the darker it is for those on the ship. As the bereaved, we're journeying refugees of grief under the umbrella of the lighthouse's illumination. After a time, we're not where we started and certainly not where we will end up. We can't bring back the old family or situation. To try to do so is to live *in* the loss and not *with* the loss. Change has occurred and must be acknowledged. When in the darkness, we are afraid that we will never see light again, but with the work of mourning, light will, indeed, come.

I began this book with the images of shell stone, coquina, and a spiral shell. The shell stone and coquina represent our being able to integrate grief into our lives through our active and purposeful mourning. The spiral shell represents a journey where we move ever upward—towards a finite point where suffering no longer is necessary. This difficult journey makes our lives stronger, which means that later we can reach our hands out to others in need. It's then, perhaps, that we can be grateful for the grief that we now own fully.

God writes straight on crooked lines

It has been said that God writes straight on crooked lines. Life provides the crooked lines upon which God can act. Eventually, we learn that what has happened had deep connections to who we have become. We never know how our lives will turn out without our loved ones until we have to learn. Likewise, only in retrospect can we understand how our lives have turned out with them in our lives. If God (or another sense of the Highest Being) guides your life, then you know that you are supposed to be on Earth and to be living—really living and not just existing—until you die. How we choose to live our lives is our best act of mourning for it is our truest memorial to our deceased loved ones.

I wish you peace in your journey.

About the Artists

Daryl Lengyel

Daryl Lengyel is a trained Minister of Consolation and leader of a Bereaved Parents USA group in Harford Country, MD. She also is a professional seamstress who has provided guidance and examples of sewing and other mourning activities for this book. Daryl is the inspiration behind *More Good Words*.

Moonjoo and Esther Lee

Moonjoo Lee painted the cover for this book. The butterfly symbolizes change of life, new beginnings, and in some traditions, it is believed to be the soul of the deceased flying free in a new life. The stone wall in this painting is the artist's representation of the *Wailing Wall* in Jerusalem. Moonjoo is a graduate of the Hongik University, a noted art college in Seoul, South Korea. She has won awards and scholarships for her artwork. Moonjoo's art is characterized by a rich integration of subject, color, and texture.

Esther Lee created the line drawings for this book's illustrations. She is in college studying art and the world.

Virginia Lee Lengyel is the sensitive artist who created the stunning *Release into Life* picture that I proudly hang in my home and enjoy in wonder.

Photographs were taken by professional photographer Robin Sommers and talented amateurs Russell J. Hewett, Bowen Lee, and Dawn Hammerbacher, as well as Beth L. Hewett.